Dear Edith...
ON REAL ESTATE

Dear Edith... on Real Estate

America's Award-Winning Columnist Answers *All* Your Questions

Edith Lank

Longman Financial Services Publishing
a division of Longman Financial Services Institute, Inc.

While a great deal of care has been taken to provide accurate and current information, the ideas, suggestions, general principles and conclusions presented in this book are subject to local, state and federal laws and regulations, court cases and any revisions of same. The reader is thus urged to consult legal counsel regarding any points of law—this publication should not be used as a substitute for competent legal advice.

Publisher: Kathleen A. Welton
Acquisitions Editor: Wendy Lochner
Senior Project Editor: Jack L. Kiburz

©1990 by Edith Lank

Published by Longman Financial Services Publishing
a division of Longman Financial Services Institute, Inc.

All rights reserved. The text of this publication, or any part thereof, may not be reproduced in any manner whatsoever without written permission from the publisher.

Printed in the United States of America

90 91 92 10 9 8 7 6 5 4 3 2 1

Library of Congress Cataloging-in-Publication Data

Lank, Edith.
    Dear Edith—on real estate : America's award-winning real estate columnist answers all your questions / by Edith Lank.
        p. cm.
ISBN 0-7931-0007-0
1. Real estate business. 2. House buying. 3. House selling. 4. Home ownership. I. Title.
HD1379.L327 1990
643′.12—dc20   89-29969
                                                                                         CIP

CONTENTS

Preface   xi

         PART 1.   HOME BUYING   1

1. *Home Buying Basics*   3
Seller Comes First • Getting Started in Buying • Buying Now or Saving More • Information out of State • Buying First Home • New Home versus Existing • How Much with Cash? • Translating Those Ads • Agent Works with Buyer • Worried about Defects • Seller Refused Offer • More Than the Asking Price • Kickback from Seller • Builder Won't Sell Lot • Buyer's Remorse Hits • Seller Keeps Deposit • Father-in-Law Asks • Paying for the Condo • Trouble at Walk-Through • Walk-Through for Closing • Getting the Sellers Out • Long Way from $941 • What about Time-Shares? • Don't Want To Be Burned • Buying Time-Share • Close To Purchasing

2. *Buying with a Partner*   15
Friends Indeed • Sharing the Rent • Buying out a Partner • Cousin Won't Buy Her Out

3. *Those Fascinating Mortgages*   17
Cash or a Mortgage? • Which Mortgage Is Best? • Misunderstands Cap • Just What's PMI? • Buying in Retirement •

Lowest Interest Rates • No Down Payment • Buying with
Nothing Down • Putting a Minimum Down • PITI 25/33,
90 L-V-R • Fluctuating Income • Lying to the Bank •
Never Borrowed Before • Income of $100,000 • Gift Letter
or Scam? • Finding the FHA • Retired at 45 • Daughter's
Drinking Problem • Too Much for FmHA • Refinancing
Farmer's Home • Shared-Equity Mortgages • Buying in
Retirement • Rates Didn't Go Down • Cosigned a Note •
Claims Good Credit • Buying after Bankruptcy • No
Income Verification • Past Credit Problems • Ex-Husband
Is a Veteran • Qualifying for VA Loan • What about Army
Reserve? • How Much Down for VA? • The VA Rider •
Veteran Is 71 • Wouldn't Take VA Buyer • Price of VA-
Mortgaged Home • Using VA in Canada • VA Eligibility
for $8,500

4. *Real Estate Investment How-To's*   33
Something about Depreciation • Renting out Half • Buy
Now for Later • Puzzled about Depreciation • Investor's
Down Payment • In Military, Going Overseas • Finding
Income Property • Taken out and Shot • Tempting Tax
Sales • Beautiful Two-Year-Old • Buying from an Estate •
Bargains from the Government • Comment on Nothing
Down • Taking a $4,500 Course • Letter I Didn't Print

5. *Landlord and Tenant*   41
Letters I Didn't Print • New Landlord and Leases •
Getting a Credit Report • Big Loss on Tenants • Landlord's
Deductible Expenses • No Key to the Apartment • Return
on Investment • Families with Children • Can Landlord
Enter? • Tenant Sublet the House • Renting in Florida •
Forced To Sign • Writing a Lease-Option • Landlord's
Eviction Technique • Rent in Advance • Addresses
Indefinite • Holdover Tenant Skipped • Bad Situation
with Landlady

PART 2. HOME OWNING — 49

6. *Home Owning—Mortgages* — 51
Not Paid Down Enough • About Equity Acceleration • Doesn't Come out Right • Lower in Off-Months • That APR Mystery • Dropping PMI Charges • Checking the Bank's Figures • Biweekly Mortgage • What's FHA Insurance for? • Mortgage Insurance or Life Insurance? • About Mortgage Insurance • Raising Escrow Payments • Unhappy with Secondary Market • Threatened VA Foreclosure

7. *Home Owning and the IRS* — 59
More about Points • Points Still Not Deductible • What To Deduct • New Rules on Interest • Deducting for Loan • Credit Union Rules • Borrowing for College • New Rules on Depreciation • Not Deductible in Texas • Repairs versus Improvements • Deducting on Vacant Land • Deducting a Lot of Interest • Deducting Son's Points

8. *Defects and Problems* — 65
Letters I Didn't Print • Electric Lines over the Pool • Buying Land out of Town • Holes in Garage Roof • Moving That Fence • FHA and the Fuse Box • Fridge in the Basement • Closing Agent Faulty • Supporting Beams Cracked • No Deed, No Nothing • Those Light Bulbs • Assessed Value Differs

9. *Decisions, Decisions* — 71
Selling and Renting • Better in the Long Run • Wouldn't Have To Move • Early Loan Payoff • Paying Off That Mortgage • Paid Off at a Discount • Couldn't Get a Discount • Documents at Payoff • Recording Mortgage Satisfaction • Who Pays for Certificate? • Loan Paid Off • $25 for a Certificate • Refinancing VA Loan • New Rule on VA Refinance • Going Price in Neighborhood • Keep It or Sell? • Improving Their Cape Cod • $600,000 Tax-Free • Taking over the House • Giving the House to Son • Why the Lawyer Did It • Federal Estate Tax Exclusion

10. *That FHA Refund* **81**
Government Owes Money • Life and Disability Insurance •
FHA Mortgage Refund • Doesn't Seem Fair • Refund of
MIP • Had an FHA Loan • Elusive FHA Insurance
Refund • Very Nice Surprise • Don't Miss FHA Refund •
Got More than He Paid • $1,200 Refund from FHA • Ran
into a Stone Wall • Where To Find FHA Case Number •
It's for Real • Becoming Refund Tracers • Yet Another
Tracer • It's a Total Rip-Off • Letters from Tracers • All
Those Wasted Stamps • No VA Refund • Paid off VA Loan •
Veteran Wants Refund • No VA Insurance • Sold with
FHA Loan

11. *Understanding Real Estate Law* **91**
What "et al." Means • Late Husband's Name • Property Is
Abandoned • Losing That Pension • House in Aunt's Name •
Has Only Life Use • Wrote in Lawyerly Words • Lawyer
Says No Will • Changing the Zoning • Difficulty Paying
the Mortgage • Son Lived in Tennessee • Can't Find Her
Deed • Son Built on His Land • Canceling the Listing •
Cabin in Canada • Trees in a Line • What Happens with
Foreclosure? • Lost the Abstract • Bought on a Land
Contract • Mother's Life Estate • Wants To Cash Out •
Would Still Owe the Money • Keeping the VA Loan •
Neighbor Moved the Stake • Chapter and Verse • What To
Do with Deed • Quit-Claim Deed • Unhappy with Title
Insurance • What Lawyers Charge • When Property
Transfers • Landlord's Hanky-Panky • Going Back to
Mother • Objects to Wording • Finding a Lawyer • Never
Got a Tax Bill • Mentioned in Will • Establishing
Ownership • Fence inside the Line • Letters I Didn't Print

PART 3. HOME SELLING **107**

12. *Selling Basics* **109**
Doing Only One Thing Wrong • Dolling up the House •
Selling for Quick Cash • Negotiating Commissions • Not a
Free Appraisal • Differing Opinion • Inflating for Private
Sale • Selling in Florida • Selling Sister's Home • Letting the

Lender Know • House Is Free and Clear • Different Sorts of Value • Selling with Furniture • Wants Market Value • Selling and Buying • Buying Off the Ex-Wife • Can't Sell in Four Years • Withdrawing in the Winter • Buyers Make Value • Seller Paying Points • Resort Lots Again • Property Zoned Commercial • Take out That Sink • Disputes Assessment Judgment • Trouble with Honest Estimates • No Standard Commission • Setting Seduction Scene • Resort Land Again • Run-Down House • Not Assessed Enough • Not One Offer • That Costly Handrail • Home Impossible To Sell • Engineer's Inspection • Selling Land in Belleville • Who Gets the $100? • Is Commission Negotiable? • Which Firm To Choose?

13. *Those Real Estate Brokers*   125
More Pregnant • Agent Paying the Rest • How Long To List • Listing with Three Brokers • Too Many Friends • Friends Drawing Straws • Just Send a Client • Buyers in a Hurry • That Microwave Oven • Broker's Flat Fee • From a Secretary • Avoiding Vicious Neighbor • Avoiding the Commission • Competing with Her Agent

14. *Real Estate as a Career*   131
Without a License • Parents Are Getting Nervous • Salesman After 60 • Finding out about Real Estate • Part-Time Trouble • What about Child Care?

15. *Seller Financing*   135
Letter I Almost Didn't Print • Unforeseen Problems • Outraged at Mortgage Default • Selling on Contract • Borrower Isn't Paying • Lent to Brother-in-Law • Mortgage at One Percent • Should She Sell? • Lender Doesn't Seem To Want Money • No Payment since 1972

16. *Assumed Mortgages*   141
Caught on FHA Assumption • Assuming VA and FHA • Assuming a VA Loan • Getting the House Back • From the Buyer's Viewpoint • New Owner Not Interested • Mess with the VA • Who Gets the Refund? • Veteran Still Liable • Ex-Husband on the Mortgage

17. *Selling and the IRS*   **147**
Deducting Interest Again • Ex-Husband's Liability • Tax Break on Second Home • Tax on Inherited Cottage • Selling Father's Cropland • Selling His Mother's Home • Because Uncle Sam Says So • Inheriting from Daughter • Tax on Gift Property • Mother Has No Will • The Ultimate Tax Shelter • Wrong 1099 Sent • IRS Report Seems Wrong • Converting Back to Own Home • Gifts to Grandchildren • Property for Services • No Receipts or Bills • December or January? • Very Important Question • Tax-Deferred Exchange • Tax Break for Disabled • Negative Amortization and IRS • Sold Home at a Loss

18. *Postponing Tax on Profit*   **157**
Within Two-Year Period • Next Home Cost Less • Replacing Summer Cottage • Remodeling the House • Off to London • Making Home Improvements • Tax Return on Selling • Living in Half the House • Was the IRS Wrong? • Investing Inherited Money • Selling the A-Frame • Investing in Tax-Free Savings • Building It Himself • Good News and Bad News • Office in Home

19. *That $125,000 Tax Break*   **163**
Commission and $125,000 • What Makes a Sale? • Nine Months a Year • Last Three Years Enough • Paying Off Loan • Renting before the Sale • Lives in One Apartment • Two-Owner Tax Break • Used the Exclusion before • Widow and Widower Marrying • Husband Did Use It • Widow and Widower Married • Husband Left no Will • Permanent Resident of Florida • Must She Sell? • How Big a Half? • Tax Break on Cottage • Marrying before Birthday • Selling Two Residences • Interest and That $125,000 • Mixed up on Tax Breaks • Plot of Land Sale • Interest Is Taxable • $38,000 Entry Fee • Federal or State Tax? • Mother Hasn't Paid Tax • Not There Three Years • Canceling the Exclusion • Dying Without Using Exclusion • Sold after the Divorce • Only One Is 55 • Letters I Didn't Print • Ingenious Proposal • Accountant's Bad Advice • Selling Two Lots • Good News on That Tax Break • Selling Two Houses

Index   **177**

PREFACE

Dear Edith: Should I put the house in my daughter's name?... How do we claim that FHA refund?... So do we wait and save more for a down payment? ...What can I do about my tenant?... How do we buy out his ex-wife?... What about that $125,000 exclusion?

For 15 years now, questions about real estate have poured in to my syndicated column, and every one receives a personal response by mail—even the ones that start "Dear Sir" and come from cities that use my picture at the head of the column! The biggest problems that people have seem to recur year after year: how to buy that first home, when to consider refinancing, how to get the best price when you sell, how to keep the IRS at bay. All are addressed here, as well as many others you may never even have thought of!

This book is more than a collection of the more interesting questions and answers we've had over the years. It furnishes an entire basic education in real estate—and painlessly. I almost called it *The Joy of Real Estate*. Real estate is fascinating and so are the lives you can glimpse through people's letters. Whether you read for information or just for fun, I do hope you'll enjoy the book.

Writing it has been extra enjoyable because of the helpful reviewers, Dr. Kenneth Edwards, Dannette Hill Lank and Esther Vail. From my publisher, encouragement came from Anita Constant, Charlie Wenk, Anne Schultz and Bobbye Middendorf, practical assistance and enthusiasm from Kathy Welton, Wendy Lochner and Jack Kiburz. Thanks are due to Vince Maselli for the photo, to the Los Angeles Times Syndicate for permission to reprint material from past columns, to Tom Flynn and John Campbell of the Rochester (NY) *Democrat & Chronicle* and to the many lawyers, accountants, editors, brokers, broadcasters and educators who have helped over the years.

My husband suggests that I extend the same invitation to readers of this book as I do to those who read the column—I'll answer your letter if you include a stamped, self-addressed return envelope. Easy for him to say—he doesn't write the letters! But it'll be fun to see how many come in and whether they differ from the newspaper queries—and I'd like your reaction to the book.

Whether you're buying, owning, selling or just reading for the joy of real estate, I wish you good luck!

Edith Lank
240 Hemingway Drive
Rochester, NY 14620

PART 1

Home Buying

"We can't get our deposit back...what did we do wrong?"

Most buyer letters come from those on their first time out. After seeing a few years of questions, I put together a college mini-course on home buying, and that resulted in my first published book, which paved the way for the radio show, which led to TV. . . . So I owe real thanks to first-time home buyers.

CHAPTER 1

Home Buying Basics

SELLER COMES FIRST

Dear Edith: What do you look for in a broker to represent you in the purchase of a home? Experience, attitude, knowledge, etc.?—A.K.

You want someone who is interested in you and your needs, who has expertise and knows the current housing market and mortgage market. You need a broker with whom you feel comfortable, one who inspires confidence.

I am disturbed, though, by your assumption that the broker represents you. Almost always, the broker is hired by the seller, is paid by the seller and represents the seller. That agency involves a special set of duties, among them an obligation to put the seller's interests first.

The agent also owes the seller other things, such as obedience and confidentiality, and is not under those particular obligations to you.

Before you panic—the agent is also required to be honest and fair with buyers. You'll receive straightforward answers to your questions and much free service. But if you want someone to represent you, work only for your side, try for a purchase at the lowest price and put your interests first, you may want to hire and pay your own "buyer's broker."

GETTING STARTED IN BUYING

Dear Edith: I decided I would like to buy a house in the spring. How do I start? Find a real estate agent, go to a bank, read the paper? How should I decide how much I can afford? What is a typical down payment?—Mr. T.K.

For a spring purchase, fall isn't too early to start reading ads, to familiarize yourself with the market. After that, contact a real estate agent by answering ads or by walking into a real estate office cold. This won't cost you anything.

Brokers are usually paid by the seller, and you have no obligation to the one you work with.

The agent will analyze your financial situation and give you an idea of what you can afford. Talking with a banker usually comes after you've found a house and settled your contract with the seller.

Depending on purchase price, type of mortgage and your individual situation, down payment can range from almost nothing to what is considered a full down payment, 20 percent. You will also need closing costs (perhaps three percent of sale price), possibly points (each point is one percent of the loan) and prepaid property taxes and insurance.

BUYING NOW OR SAVING MORE

Dear Edith: My husband and I have been renting. Our rent was just increased, and we expect it will go up again next year. We had planned to stay here and rent for about four years to save enough for a hefty down payment on a house but we are wondering if it would be to our advantage to buy something temporarily until we are able to afford our dream house. — Mrs. N.L.

Forget about waiting four years. By all means, buy whatever you can afford right now, and then start saving for your dream home.

INFORMATION OUT OF STATE

Dear Edith: We will be moving out of state within the next year. How does one look for a home in a totally unfamiliar area? How do we check out school districts, the makeup of neighborhoods (young areas with children, etc.)? — Mrs. S.S.

Subscribe to the out-of-town newspaper for a couple of months. You can learn a great deal about neighborhoods by paying close attention to local news and classified ads.

Because they are concerned about unintentionally violating fair housing laws, many real estate brokers hesitate to give you their opinion on school systems and other characteristics of neighborhoods. You can always ask, though, for factual information — per-pupil expenditure in various districts; the availability of foreign language study programs, computers, libraries and music instruction; the number of graduates going on to four-year institutions; and the like. As for a neighborhood with young children, do some driving around after school is out, to see for yourself.

BUYING FIRST HOME

Dear Edith: My husband and I are first-time homebuyers, 23 years of age, no children. The price they are asking for the house we like is only half what I saw a similar house for elsewhere. But we asked the broker if the seller of the house we want would move on the price. He said the seller would not move on the price. Question number 1. Do many people end up paying full price? After we signed the contracts a friend said you are not supposed to pay list price. Were we taken advantage of? 2. They told us one interest rate on our mortgage and then mentioned an APR rate that was 3/4 of a percent more. Does this mean we are not getting the original rate?

Your advice and suggestions would be appreciated. Comments from my friends are negative and make me feel worse. — Mrs. S.A.

Don't let your friends bother you. Buying whatever you can afford at this point is an excellent way to get started building up some equity.

The price of a similar house in a different location is no guide to value. What counts is how much houses are bringing in the same neighborhood. Now as for your specific questions:

1. Many houses sell at the listing price, and a few even above it. The fact that you are getting a new mortgage loan offers some protection because a bank appraiser must agree that the house is worth what you are paying.
2. The APR (annual precentage rate) figure takes into account your yearly rate, which is the one originally quoted, and also the points charged, which represent additional interest.

NEW HOME vs. EXISTING

Dear Edith: My husband and I plan to move in a year or two to a larger house. What are the pros and cons of buying an existing house compared to building a new one? — H.K.

When you buy an existing home, you pretty much know what it will cost and when you will get it. Of course, what you get may not be exactly what you'd prefer. When you build from scratch, you get to choose things just the way you want them. That's the big plus; it also accounts for some of the minuses.

Making those choices requires a big investment of time and effort on your part. The need to make one decision after another can put a strain on your emotions — and on your marriage.

Building does offer creative satisfaction, but you must be prepared for plenty of discussion, argument and frustration. Most people who build report that the process required much more time — and sometimes more money — than they had expected to invest.

HOW MUCH WITH CASH?

Dear Edith: How much could one save by offering full cash for an older home or fixer-up?—Mrs. F.I.

An all-cash offer usually warrants some price concession. Every transaction is different, though, and every seller's situation unique, so there's no specific answer to your question.

TRANSLATING THOSE ADS

Dear Edith: My wife and I are looking to buy our first home. We don't have a lot of money for a large down payment. We always see ads stating "assume payments." Can you explain what this means? Will it require a down payment, and if so, how much? What about "Will hold the mortgage, you assume payments, principals only"? Does that mean a credit check is not required? And "creative financing." Does it really work? Would it be something we should look into?—Mr. S.K.

Sometimes the mortgage presently on a house can be taken over (assumed) by the next owner. Certain mortgages are assumable; others are not and must be paid off when the property is sold.

Is a credit check required? With "freely assumable" mortgages (some FHAs and VAs) it is not. Other mortgages (some adjustable rate mortgages, newer FHAs and VAs) are "assumable with lender's approval," and the buyer must qualify as to credit, other debts and income.

As for down payment: suppose a house is worth $90,000, and has on it an assumable mortgage with a balance of $60,000. You could take the loan along with the house at a considerable saving of time, paperwork and closing costs. But in order to do so, you'd have to give the seller the rest of the purchase price, $30,000, in cash.

Sometimes the seller will accept a smaller down payment, perhaps $5,000, and let you pay the rest month by month on a second mortgage for $25,000. In that case you'd have two monthly payments to meet. That's probably what's happening in your "Will hold mortgage, you assume payments" ad.

If the sellers are going to hold a mortgage, they'd be foolish to do so without asking for a credit check.

"Principals only" means that a seller wants to deal directly with buyers and does not want to hear from brokers. When it comes to home buying, you are a principal in the transaction.

As for creative financing, that term can cover all sorts of unusual arrangements. Before you accept any creative proposal, have your own lawyer or accountant look it over.

AGENT WORKS WITH BUYER

Dear Edith: Would you please give me some information on how important it is to have a lawyer that will work with you when you are ready to buy a home? I want to pass it on to my son. He feels he doesn't need one because the agent works with you.—Mrs. W.E.

Your son is right: the real estate agent does work *with* the buyer, who receives honest, straightforward assistance and many free services. But the agent does not work *for* the buyer. A broker is (usually) paid by the seller and, when push comes to shove, owes first loyalty to the seller.

No matter what local custom dictated, I would never buy anything, anywhere, without my own real estate attorney, someone entirely on my side. For one thing, before laying out a large amount of money I'd want assurance that I was buying clear, trouble-free title, and that's a legal opinion no broker is qualified to give.

WORRIED ABOUT DEFECTS

Dear Edith: How can I find out if there are any hidden defects in property before I decide to buy?—Mr. T.D.

A good way to protect yourself is to ask the seller, preferably in front of witnesses, "Do you know of any hidden defects I should be aware of before I decide about buying?" The seller owes you an honest answer. So does a real estate broker.

If you are willing to invest in a professional building inspection by an engineer, you can make your offer to purchase "subject to a satisfactory engineering report." You would engage the engineer only after your purchase offer had been accepted in writing.

SELLER REFUSED OFFER

Dear Edith: We wrote an offer on a house on Sunday morning, but the agent couldn't get ahold of the sellers to present it. By the time the sellers came home, another offer had been written (after dinner) and they accepted that one. It wasn't our fault they were out all day, and we feel they should have dealt with our offer first—made us a counter-offer at least, so we'd have had the chance we were entitled to.—Ms. B.G.

Sorry, but when several offers come in, the one that was written first doesn't have any priority. It's proper to let the sellers see all offers at once, and deal with whichever they choose.

MORE THAN THE ASKING PRICE

Dear Edith: After looking at a house a second time, I told my agent I would like to make an offer on it the next day. That evening my agent said the listing agent had told her that there was another "very good" offer being prepared. My agent suggested I write a contract immediately before the other one could be presented.

Instead of trying to offer the price and terms I wanted, I was convinced that in order to have my offer accepted, I should offer $500 over the asking price. This was accepted by the sellers.

What are the chances that either agent duped me?—E.K.N.

Slim.

It really is sometimes advisable to make an offer for more than the asking price, particulary when property is newly listed at a no-nonsense figure.

Of course I can't know whether any particular person is honest, but consider this: by the time the commission was divided among listing office, listing agent, selling office and selling agent, "your" agent probably stood to make about $7 if you paid $500 more. Hardly seems worth lying about.

Neither one was your agent, by the way, unless you had specifically hired a buyer's broker. Both were working for the seller. Both agents had special legal obligations to the seller, including obtaining the best price for the house. They were also, however, required by law to deal honestly with buyers.

KICKBACK FROM SELLER

Dear Edith: My fiancee and I plan to purchase a starter home this year. I expect we'll be relatively "cash-poor" following our closing date.

A number of friends have suggested we get an agreement on the purchase price, then suggest to the seller that he write a contract for $5,000 over the purchase price. The seller then writes us a check for $5,000. Do you feel this is a wise method to improve post-closing-date cash flow problems?—Mr. K.D.

It's not wise, but it sure is illegal. What kind of friends do you have? What goes on in your town anyhow?

Fraud of that sort means everyone must lie to the lending institution—seller, lawyers, real estate brokers and most of all yourselves. (The maximum penalty for perjury to a federally chartered institution is two years in prison.)

On the other hand, there's no violation of law if the seller agrees to pay part of your closing costs or points toward your mortgage loan. Such an agreement would be clearly stated in your contract, out in the open for all to see.

BUILDER WON'T SELL LOT

Dear Edith: I wish to purchase a lot in a development area where the houses will sell for $175,000 and up. I would like to build a house of my own design, using "sweat equity" with a builder friend of mine, that would conform with other houses in that area but only cost me around $95,000.

The builder who owns the development says he will only sell to me if he does the building. Is there any way I can buy that lot and build my own house?—R.A.

Builders have every right to reserve their land for their own customers. There's nothing you can do about it.

BUYER'S REMORSE HITS

Dear Edith: I am writing you in the middle of the night. We put an offer in to buy our first home last Sunday, and the sellers accepted it right away. Now we're having second thoughts, and our lawyer says we are legally bound to buy. Is this really so? Please answer as soon as possible. I've had to start taking sleeping pills.—Ms. L.S.

Sounds like a classic attack of the malady known as Buyer's Remorse.

First-time home buyers are at greatest risk for this disease. Onset is usually from 24 hours to two weeks after a purchase offer is accepted. Symptoms develop rapidly around 2 A.M., as you lie awake wondering why you ever got into this, if you can really afford the house, and whether the whole thing isn't a Big Mistake. Buyer's Remorse is akin to the last-minute jitters that afflict brides and grooms before the wedding.

Rather than lose any more sleep, call your real estate broker right now, and ask if you can visit the house again, preferably when the sellers are away. "Measuring for curtains" is a logical pretext; no need to alarm the owners.

In nearly every instance, buyers are pleasantly reassured during a return visit. You're likely to find that all your house-hunting and research really did pay off, that this is clearly the best house for you.

If, as happens rarely, you are more depressed than ever after you've viewed the house again, then it's time for another conference with your lawyer, to determine how much money you stand to forfeit by backing out.

SELLER KEEPS DEPOSIT

Dear Edith: If the buyer is approved for financing and still backs out of buying a house, does the seller get to keep the deposit?—Mr. R.F.

Yes.

That's a bold statement to make without having seen the sale contract or heard the whole story. But usually the buyer who backs out for no good reason forfeits the deposit and may owe additional damages.

FATHER-IN-LAW ASKS

Dear Edith: My youngest son and his future wife are buying their first home. They were told they could rent out the basement apartment in this split-level if they also bought the two acres behind the house.

Now comes the story. The land isn't quite two acres, they are not sure the apartment can legally be rented, there is no reduction in the price and the closing date is being changed. My son had an engineer look over the house; he will need a new roof. Also, the water may have a problem.

Personally, I would drop the whole deal. They are both green and I hate to see them get rooked. —Mr. N.F.

Contracts are binding; that's what they're for. One doesn't always have the option of dropping the whole deal without incurring penalties.

Green kids—and anyone else—should have their own lawyer's input before a contract becomes firm. Did the contract specify exactly two acres, was the place held out in the contract as a legal duplex, was the purchase subject to a satisfactory engineer's report?

An attorney can look over the contract and tell your son where he stands now.

PAYING FOR THE CONDO

Dear Edith: Our condo is partway completed, and they are asking us for more cash. There is a clause in our purchase agreement that various sums are to be paid upon completion of certain items, like basement dug, roughing in building, drywall, etc., but I don't feel this is valid. Can you advise us of our course of action? —Mr. S.T.

You can't make a contract invalid just by wishing it were so. What grounds do you have? The time to object was before you signed the agreement.

My guess is that you are legally bound to live up to your promises. You owe whatever sums you agreed to pay.

TROUBLE AT WALK THROUGH

Dear Edith: My son put a deposit on a house but when the walk through came just before closing he found many things wrong, some major, some minor. What can he do to protect himself or to have these things taken care of? —Mr. A.F.

You know the standard lawyer's answer: "It all depends."

Were the problems readily visible when your son first looked at the house? Did the purchase contract provide that he'd take the place "as is" or did the seller promise everything would be in working order? Has the property already changed hands?

If your son has not yet closed on the house, he may be able to raise some objections or ask for financial concessions. If he went ahead with the closing, the general rule in some areas is "you bought it, you got it." Whether a lawyer can achieve something after closing depends on the law in your son's state, the wording of the contract and the nature of the defects.

WALK-THROUGH FOR CLOSING

Dear Edith: We are buying a new home (well, new to us) and will have a final walk-through just before closing. What sort of things are we looking for? —Mr. D.K.

Take your sale contract along, to see if the seller is leaving everything promised: carpeting, window blinds, whatever. Check for damage that may have occured since you originally viewed the house: newly broken windows, for example. And you should receive the place in "broom-clean" condition, without piles of old newspapers or dead appliances in the attic or cellar.

GETTING THE SELLERS OUT

Dear Edith: When we bought our house, we gave the sellers 90 days to get out. Then they refused to move because their new house was not completed. We ended up taking them to court but they stalled long enough to avoid eviction.

What could we have done to encourage them to leave on time? —Mr. S.K.

It's best to anticipate problems like yours and head them off in advance. Your contract could have contained a move-in agreement that made it uncomfortably costly for tne sellers to remain beyond the term agreed upon.

Instead of giving them the entire purchase price at closing, you could have placed a large chunk in escrow with a third party holding it. The agreement would have provided that their rent went up sharply if they did not vacate after the 90 days. Rent would then be deducted from that escrowed sum, which would be given to them only after they moved out.

That way, they'd have had a financial incentive to leave as promised.

LONG WAY FROM $941

Dear Edith: When I got my mortgage commitment, they told me it was for 11.5 percent fixed rate with my monthly payment at $941. Then when we closed *they told me it was 12 percent. And my payment was $1,143. That's a long way from $941. My lawyer said I should close anyhow so I did. What should I do now? Here is a copy of the papers so you can see.—W.W.*

Your papers look all right to me. Let me try to explain.

First, the difference in percentage. According to the papers, your commitment was for 11.5 percent, and the "annual percentage rate" quoted on your statement is 11.73, not 12. The 11.73 represents your original 11.5, with additional closing costs and payment of points taken into account. Annual percentage rate is something that confuses many people, but it doesn't mean you're really paying more than was quoted.

You didn't send me any statement about that $1,143 payment, but I suspect that what has happened is this: you are still sending in $941 a month for principal and interest on your loan. The rest is for one month's saving toward next year's property taxes and home-owners insurance bills. The lender will get those bills and pay them out of the extra money you send in each month.

WHAT ABOUT TIME-SHARES?

Dear Edith: Will you please write on the pros and cons of a time-share vacation home? I understand if I make a $3,000 payment I can use it every year for two weeks, plus maintenance while I'm there. As I'm not sure what I want to do, would appreciate your advice in a column.—I.S.

In most cases, a time share is a poor investment. Owners can seldom get their money out when they go to sell. If you are sure you want to vacation in the same spot every year, try to buy a used one on the resale market. You may be able to pick up a bargain from someone who has to sell at a loss.

DON'T WANT TO BE BURNED

Dear Edith: We purchased our Florida time-share in 1983 and have been satisfied, but because of declining health we are eager to sell but we don't want to be burned. I should appreciate your advice.—L.C.E.

Real estate brokers aren't eager to list time-shares, because their low prices don't yield enough commission to cover the time and money expended. Advertise the place yourself in local newspapers near the unit.

You can't be the only ones with a time-share to sell in that area. There is probably a more or less standard price, and it's whatever the buying public is ready to pay. Reading other ads in those local newspapers should give you an idea of market value.

BUYING TIME-SHARE

Dear Edith: Now that our children are married and through school we would like to spend winter vacations (a week or so) in Florida. A few of our friends have time-share condos with one particular development and seem fairly happy though some feel yearly fees, etc., are high.

Your article a couple of weeks ago discouraged buying new time-share condos, but how do you feel about second-hand ones? Are there listings? Is there a typical price range for a one-week, prime-time used condo?—N. and T.O.

I have no special information about the group you mention, and there are no typical prices except in a particular development.

You'd want to talk with others who owned in any development, to get a general feeling before you bought. If your friends have had good experiences, that's significant. But in general, as you know, I'm skeptical. If you know you want the same week in the same place every year—maybe. If you want it as an investment, or you count on exchanging for other areas—better think twice.

And by all means investigate the price of resale units before buying a new one from the developer.

CLOSE TO PURCHASING

Dear Edith: Recently we came close to purchasing from the developer a time-share at a resort. We backed out after we talked to four current owners who were advertising their time shares for resale. Each was asking less than originally paid, in one case the decrease was substantial.

How can I find out what actual prices on resale have been, as opposed to "asking prices"?—T.E.N.

If the time-shares are being sold as real estate, you should be able to find the sales in the public records, which anyone can inspect. Ask at the county clerk's office where the resort is located. Real estate agents in that area may have information also.

CHAPTER 2

Buying with a Partner

Recent years have brought me questions about joint ownership, as the makeup of the average home buyer changes. More single parents out there, but also more unrelated couples. As for related owners—those with harmonious relationships don't write to the newspapers. Sometimes my mail seems to indicate that no one in this whole country gets along with relatives.

FRIENDS INDEED

Dear Edith: My friend and I are both employed and have good credit. We intend to buy a house together. Do you have any advice about pitfalls?—Ms. R.L.

Discuss ahead of time all the "what-ifs." What if one of you becomes unemployed? Moves out of town? Gets married? Disagrees about whether repairs are needed? Wants to move out and rent half the house to a tenant? Has a friend who needs somewhere to live for a while? For good?

How will you determine price if one of you someday buys out the other?

And what would you want to happen if one of you died? Should that person's share go automatically to the other, or would you want it left in the estate, to go to other heirs?

Determine these things now, while you can do it calmly and without emotion. Then go together to an attorney and have your agreement set down on paper to head off problems in advance.

SHARING THE RENT

Dear Edith: My sister and I own a duplex. She and her husband live in one side, the other side is rented out. I believe I am entitled to the rent we receive; she thinks she should share in this income.—Mrs. F.L.

You're right; she's wrong. Expenses (taxes, repairs and the like) should be shared between you. So should rental income, but only if she pays full market rental for her side.

BUYING OUT A PARTNER

Dear Edith: I own a townhouse with another person. If one of us wanted to sell our half-interest to the other, how do we decide on the fair market value of the townhouse? If the one needs to place a new loan or second loan in order to buy the other out, what would be involved?—Mr. K.T.

Owners in your situation often pay several hundred dollars for a couple of professional appraisals, with an agreement ahead of time to average the two estimates and use that figure for selling price. The transfer can usually be handled with minimal paperwork by a real estate attorney.

A new mortgage would be judged like any other loan. It would depend on the debt presently on the property, the value of the townhouse, and the financial qualifications of the borrower.

COUSIN WON'T BUY HER OUT

Dear Edith: My cousin and I own a house our grandfather willed to us. He moved in and has been there five years now. He agreed to buy me out; I sent over an appraiser and asked for my half. But he keeps making excuses. What legal steps could I take to settle this situation?—Ms. F.K.N.

Unless you're charging rent for the use of your half, your cousin has no motivation to buy you out, and every reason to stall.

You have the right to force a public sale of the property (court order for partition). Problem is, such a sale may not bring full value, and lawsuits cost money.

An attorney is the one to advise you about what steps to take. If you're lucky, a simple lawyer's letter will light a fire under your cousin, without any court action needed.

CHAPTER 3

Those Fascinating Mortgages

"We've never borrowed so we have no credit..."

Which mortgage plan is best? What's P.I.T.I.? And over and over, "Can we get a mortgage loan after a bankruptcy?" Lots of questions come in about how to qualify for a loan, about VA entitlement, and buying after retirement.

CASH OR A MORTGAGE?

Dear Edith: What is the best way to purchase a home the first time? Pay cash or get a mortgage and use interest paid as an income tax deduction?—N.O.

The answer depends on your total financial situation, your other assets and what use you'd make of the money if you didn't buy for cash. If you take out a loan, you'll be paying deductible interest, but at the same time the money you didn't put into the house might be earning taxable income for you somewhere else.

Don't let income tax considerations dictate your decision. These days there's a fairly high standard deduction you can always take if you choose.

What it all adds up to—there's no one answer that's right for everyone.

WHICH MORTGAGE IS BEST?

Dear Edith: I have recently sold my house and have contracted to build a new one. I will have about $60,000 cash to work with and plan on living in the new house for at least ten years. With all the choices in mortgages today, it is hard to decide which is best: fixed, adjustable, adjustable transferable, bi-weekly etc. The builder's real estate broker has referred me to a mortgage *representative at a bank. I would like your opinion on what is the best option before I talk with this person.* —*Mr. F.K.*

Asking which is the best mortgage is like going into a shoe store and asking for the best pair. The back room is filled with boxes because each shoe fits a different person and a different purpose.

Lenders offer hundreds of different mortgage plans because each fits a need: a particular house, a special time frame, seller's financial situation and buyer's qualifications. Biweekly mortgages, for example, usually involve automatic transfer of funds from your bank account, which might or might not suit you.

The bank's representative should have advice on which plan fits your needs best.

MISUNDERSTANDS CAP

Dear Edith: I was offered an adjustable rate mortgage based on the current rate of interest on T-bills, plus a margin of 2 percent with a cap of 3 percent. This means that if T-bills are selling for 7 percent, my rate would be 7 percent plus 2 percent plus 3 percent, or 12 percent interest, right? —*Mr. V.M.*

Wrong.

The bank will charge you the T-bill rate, plus the margin, an extra 2 percent for its expenses and profit. The 3 percent cap means simply that no matter how much T-bill rates might skyrocket between one adjustment and the next, your interest could never go up by more than 3 percent.

In the example you give, you would start out at 9 percent—the T-bill rate plus the margin, 7 percent plus 2 percent.

Then, let's suppose that your loan is to be adjusted a year from now, and that T-bill rates have shot up to 11 percent. Your new rate should be 11 percent plus the margin, 2 percent, for a total of 13 percent. But wait—the cap comes into play. You were at 9 percent this year. The cap means your rate cannot be raised more than 3 percent at a time, so the lender would have to settle for 12 percent.

JUST WHAT'S PMI?

Dear Edith: My son purchased a house last year. A portion of his monthly payment is for PMI. Exactly what is it? Principle Mortgage Insurance? Or whatever? And is it a tax-deductible expense like the interest? —*Mr. C.S.*

Private mortgage insurance protects your son's lending institution against loss if it ever took back the property and sold it. On one's own home, the premiums are not income-tax-deductible.

BUYING IN RETIREMENT

Dear Edith: My wife and I are saving to buy a small home when we retire. We'll both be over 60. What will be our chances of getting a mortgage? Would purchasing title insurance insure our procuring this mortgage?—Mr. H.H.

Title insurance protects the lending institution (and you, depending on what type of policy you buy) against claims by someone who might dispute your ownership. Many mortgage plans do require title insurance these days, but that's not what helps you qualify for the loan.

No matter what your age, you must prove willingness to pay debts on time (good credit record) and enough income to carry the payments comfortably. Retirement income and Social Security payments count just fine toward the latter requirement.

LOWEST INTEREST RATES

Dear Edith: I would like to know how I can go about finding the lowest interest rate for a mortgage. —Mr. K.H.

Finding the lowest rate is harder than it sounds. Many adjustable rate mortgages start off low but don't stay that way very long. To compare them, you have to know how often they will be adjusted, and to what standards.

Even fixed-rate mortgages have to be judged not by the simple interest rate, but also by how many points (extra up-front interest) are being charged. To help you judge, ask about APR, annual percentage rate, which takes extra charges into consideration. It helps you compare different plans.

NO DOWN PAYMENT

Dear Edith: Is it really possible to buy a house with no cash down payment? If so, could you please tell me how to do it?—Mrs. E.

One way is to find a seller willing to take back financing—in effect, lending you the whole amount needed to purchase. Sometimes you can assume a present mortgage and find a seller willing to lend you the rest of the purchase price on a second mortgage. Few sellers, though, are willing to sign over their homes on such relatively risky terms.

If you have good credit, sufficient income and few other debts, you might qualify for a loan under a government plan:

- Buy with a nothing-down Veterans Administration mortgage (eligible veterans only).
- Buy through the FHA-221 program (families only, very modest homes).

- Buy through Farmers Home Administration (modest homes in rural areas).

That's quite a list of "ifs," but yes, there really are some no-down-payment programs available, and real estate brokers know whether they will work in any given area.

BUYING WITH NOTHING DOWN

Dear Edith: We recently tried to purchase a home with the owner holding a second mortgage so we were getting in with no money down. Wonderful idea, right? Wrong. At closing the bank pulled back the mortgage money because they found out about the second mortgage. The sellers then sued us and we settled out of court at our lawyer's advice. Are owner-held second mortgages illegal in any way?—Mrs. H.B.

Only when they involve lying to a lending institution about where your down payment is coming from.

PUTTING A MINIMUM DOWN

Dear Edith: My question is about down payments on my first home. I have been told minimum down by a lot of people, because of the tax break. Even if someone has a lot of money to put down with still some left over for emergency, should you still go with minimum down?—Mr. E.C.

Not necessarily. No one answer is right for everyone. It all depends on individual circumstances. Tax consequences don't make much difference and shouldn't enter into your decision—just take my word for it.

PITI 25/33, 90 L-V-R

Dear Edith: Someone recently gave me a list of mortgage plans from a local bank, and it included the following baffling statement: "PITI 28/36, 25/33 90 L-V-R." Can you explain?—P.I.

Here's a translation: The figures refer to the top amount the lender considers it safe for you to spend on housing cost. The PITI comes from the initials of four items included in housing cost: Principal and Interest on loan, property Taxes and Insurance.

For mortgages with a substantial down payment (at least 10 percent) the lender will allow you to spend up to 28 percent of your gross monthly income, or 36 percent of what's left including your other debt payments. That's the 28/36. Most lenders compute it both ways, and then to be conservative allow you only whichever figure is lower.

If you put less than 10 percent down, however, you are borrowing more than 90 percent of the value of the property. This gives you a loan-to-value ratio greater than 90 percent (90 L-V-R). In that case, many lenders are more restrictive. To keep you from getting in over your head, they may say you can spend only 25 percent of your gross income, or 33 percent after other debt payments have been subtracted.

When many different mortgage plans are being described and space is at a premium, the three paragraphs above can be summarized as you saw them.

FLUCTUATING INCOME

Dear Edith: I am a commission salesperson on fluctuating income. Does that make it harder to get a mortgage?—Ms. O.P.

Not necessarily. Lenders will ask to see not only a statement from your employer, but also copies of your last two income tax returns.

LYING TO THE BANK

Dear Edith: A real estate salesperson has prepared a purchase agreement for me to buy real estate stating an inflated purchase price, with a separate side agreement (which would not be disclosed to the bank) whereby the seller agrees to give me a "credit" that really results in a lower price. The salesperson indicates that this may result in a higher bank appraisal so I won't need to carry mortgage insurance which the bank would require if we used the real price in the contract. The salesperson says this is a common and acceptable practice, but my attorney advises that this is fraud and refuses to represent me in such a transaction. What is your opinon?—A.B.

Acceptable? Good grief, no. Common? I certainly hope not. Fraud? You bet.

Lying to a lending institution constitutes perjury, and the possible penalty includes two years in prison. Besides, if the bank found out they'd surely call in the whole loan immediately—which might make as much trouble for you as two years in prison.

Stay away from that salesperson—in fact, from that whole brokerage company, because it's hard to believe the supervising broker doesn't know about this shady practice. It could get you into all kinds of trouble; your lawyer doesn't want to be mixed up in it, and neither should you.

NEVER BORROWED BEFORE

Dear Edith: We would like to buy a smaller house. Our concern is that we have never bought anything on time, although our credit is excellent. We would

*like to buy before we sell. Are we going to have difficulty getting a loan?
—Mrs. L.B.*

If you don't have bad credit, you have good credit. It's not true that you need to take out a loan and pay it back promptly just to establish a credit record.

How much you can borrow depends on your income and other debts; evidently you have none so that's a plus. Talk with loan officers at a couple of lending institutions; they'll tell you where you stand.

These days some lenders let you you qualify for a loan up to a given amount even before you start your house-hunting; this makes your purchase offer particularly attractive to a seller.

INCOME OF $100,000

Dear Edith: How can a home buyer calculate what priced home he/she can afford based on annual gross income? Is there a simple formula used by brokers? Based on a 20 percent down payment at 10 percent fixed interest, can a couple with no debts and an income of $100,000 afford a $100,000, $200,000, $300,000 or $400,000 home?—I. and K.M.

Where does a big elephant sit? Anywhere it wants.

And it sounds as if you can buy just about anything you want. Depending on property taxes on the particular house, my guess is that you could go at least to $300,000.

Brokers estimate using the same criteria the bank will use. Stop in at any real estate office and ask for a financial analysis; they'll welcome you with open arms.

GIFT LETTER OR SCAM?

Dear Edith: Due to our daughter's desire to buy a house and not having a proper down payment, we are being asked to give her a paper indicating that we are going to give her a gift of $5,000. She says it doesn't mean we have to part with the money. She says the lender will accept it in "good faith."

Could you please tell us if this is just some kind of scam? Seems to us like an old-fashioned I.O.U.—L.S.

The lending institution doesn't want your daughter getting in over her head with additional borrowing elsewhere. So she's telling them extra cash for the down payment is coming from you—not with an I.O.U. but as a gift, with no repayment expected.

The paper you're being asked to sign is known as a gift letter, and it's been said that "*gift letter* is a term that has come to mean any lie in print."

Some lenders, by the way, will ask for proof that you have $5,000 available to give her.

FINDING THE FHA

Dear Edith: Where does one go to get an FHA loan? Do banks handle these as well as conventional loans? There is no FHA listing anywhere in my phone book. I would also like to get an FHA appraisal on a property but don't know where to go. Your answer to these probably stupid questions would be appreciated. —Mr. L.R.

I feel strongly that there are no stupid questions. In my real estate classes, if someone asks about the matter I just finished discussing, I figure either my explanation was inadequate, or I'm not managing to keep people awake.

The Federal Housing Administration is found under United States Government listings, and then under the Department of Housing and Urban Development. Not every town has an office, however.

The FHA does not lend money directly. Rather, it administers a mortgage insurance system for loans made through local lending institutions. Some of your local banks, savings and loans, and mortgage bankers probably handle FHA loans.

You can order an FHA appraisal through any approved lender.

RETIRED AT 45

Dear Edith: I'm 45 years old, retired on social security, and collect a pension from civil service. I was retired because of implantation of a pacemaker. I receive $24,000 a year. Because of my physical conditon, would it be difficult to be considered eligible for a mortgage?—Mr. B.

No. The lender is allowed to consider only the value of the property and your ability to repay the loan. Your pacemaker shouldn't enter into the picture. You'll be judged on the same basis as any other applicant.

DAUGHTER'S DRINKING PROBLEM

Dear Edith: I've been widowed a little over a year. Though I felt I would be all right with the three thousand dollars in my bank account, my finances were used up to spare my daughter's drinking problems. I now have a home paid up, one thousand dollars in a CD, and $200 in my savings account.

I am desperately in debt, owing more than $3,000 to Visa and $1,000 to Sears. Is it possible for me at 68 years old to get a mortgage on the house? It is worth about $60,000. Forgot to mention, my income is $808. —Mrs. B.I.

You're in luck—no bank will make you a mortgage loan.

Before you could borrow on the house, you'd have to prove you could handle monthly repayment comfortably—and you couldn't.

The last thing you need is a debt against your house. Forget about borrowing more money. It's not the way out of your troubles. Hold on to the house; keep it free and clear. Guard your remaining savings, and let your daughter worry about herself. You haven't a penny to spare and you are in real danger.

Consumer credit counseling agencies offer just the guidance you need immediately. If there's such an group in your town, call them as soon as possible. The local welfare office can usually direct you to such a non-profit agency; beware of the quick-fix money-making companies that promise to cure your problems for a large fee.

TOO MUCH FOR FmHA

Dear Edith: Recently I attended a Farmers Home Loan seminar in which I was told I could qualify for a low-interest loan if I earn $18,500 or under that amount. I am a qualified auto mechanic and earn $19,500 per year, one thousand over their limit. I am credit free even though I have two children. I have saved $4,000 toward my dream of owning my own home.

Brokers tell me I might be able to afford something in the city but I want to live in a rural area and I can't afford to with a regular loan. Is there any special program for someone who earns, say, between $19,000 and $25,000? —Mr. S.A.

Go back to the Farmers Home Administration office and ask some more questions. The dollar limit is for adjusted income. By the time they've allowed for the number of children in your family, you should qualify for a loan.

REFINANCING FARMERS HOME

Dear Edith: My home is financed through the Farmers Home Administration. We bought it in 1978 at 8 percent. Our mortgage says we may be asked to refinance at a future date.

Recently we received a letter requesting information on our finances and telling us they would like to discuss our refinancing with someone else. I checked with a bank and the interest is higher and they charge closing costs. I would like to keep the loan I presently have.

Can they force me to refinance? I have $7,000 in savings but feel I need it as we have two children who will hopefully go to college some day. Our annual income is now $47,000. —Mr. V.T.

Farmers Home Administration (FmHA) loans are intended for the purchase of homes in rural areas by those who can't qualify at regular lending institutions. The money comes directly from the Department of Agriculture.

When you took out the loan, you promised that when and if your financial situation improved, you'd place a mortgage elsewhere, so the money you borrowed could be freed up for other home buyers.

Of course you'd like to hold on to the present loan, but you'll have to cooperate in the analysis of your finances and live up to the provisions of your mortgage.

SHARED-EQUITY MORTGAGES

Dear Edith: Recently I read an article and if I understood it properly, an investor will co-sign on a mortgage note for investment purposes only. The other buyer will actually live in the house and pay the monthly note. The benefit would be for a person that wants a home but does not have the immediate funds.

Can you give me more information and direct me to some individual investors I could talk to?—Mr. B.K.

Shared-equity mortgages can be helpful in certain situations, but you'd want to work closely with your own attorney. With some arrangements, for example, you might have to buy the investor out at a certain point. If you couldn't, the place would be sold.

You'd want some protection if your co-investor went bankrupt or had judgments placed against the property, so you'd research his credit and finances just as he would research yours. You'd need an agreement on responsibility for repairs, insurance and taxes. And if property dropped in value, as it has recently in the oil-dependent states, both parties could get hurt.

The lawyer who guided you through all this might know of a party who's looking for something like that. Otherwise, try a classified ad, asking for a shared-equity investor.

BUYING IN RETIREMENT

Dear Edith: We have lived in this lovely double for 27 years. Now the owner is going to live with his son. They have offered us this house at a great price, in consideration of the work we have done on it and care we gave the owner through many illnesses.

Naturally we don't want to pull up stakes. What we pay now in rent, plus what we could get for the other side, would take care of the mortgage, taxes and other bills.

But being retired is the problem. A lawyer friend told us no bank would grant us a mortgage with an income of just under $1,500 monthly. Actually we live very nicely on that amount, save a little and take a vacation every year. Do you see any way we could buy the house?—B.D.F.

First, have you talked with the owner about taking back a mortgage? Perhaps he would be just as happy to receive monthly checks and have the mortgage as an asset to leave to his son eventually.

Then—there's no harm in talking with a couple of lending institutions. They will consider as part of your monthly income some or even all of the rent you could collect for the other side. That might bring your income high enough to qualify for a loan.

RATES DIDN'T GO DOWN

Dear Edith: Last spring I applied for refinancing my home. I dragged my feet in hopes that rates would go down. They haven't. I paid $675 (appraisal fee, credit check and half the origination fee). I don't want to go through with the loan. Would I get my $675 back?—D. LeD.

Money has already been spent for the appraisal and credit check. As for the other fee, the answer lies in the papers you signed when you applied for the loan. My guess is that you agreed to forfeit the money if you didn't close.

COSIGNED A NOTE

Dear Edith: If you have cosigned a note for someone, is this taken into consideration when they review your credit report, income and other qualifications for a mortgage?—Mrs. O.C.

Certainly. When you cosigned, you took on contingent responsibility for that other debt. A lending institution would consider it in analyzing your financial obligations.

CLAIMS GOOD CREDIT

Dear Edith: My wife and I have good income and a good credit record. We have a lot of normal debts, and banks have rejected us for mortgage loans because of our debt load. We also have a judgment that I am unwilling to pay because of philosophical differences.

We'd like a big loan to consolidate our debts, but cannot tap into the equity on our house. But my mother's house is free and clear and I'm going to own it some day anyhow.

She tried to borrow for us but her social security and small pension won't meet the payment requirements. Is there a way we could go through the paperwork to get it in my name, with her paying rent, taxes and everything reported to make it legal but not paying anything in real dollars? As long as the net result would be to have the house in our name. Mom is all for it if it will help and there are no legal consequences.—Mr. K.E.

The best thing your mother can do for you is hold on to that house in her own name and keep it debt-free.

When you have a judgment outstanding and have been turned down for a mortgage, you're stretching things to claim good credit. And your debt load isn't normal if lending institutions say you have too many payments.

If you can't qualify for a loan on your own house, you won't do any better on your mother's unless you lie about rental income (and pay off that judgment, of course). It's dangerous to perjure your way into more debt than lending institutions feel you're qualified for.

Locate your local nonprofit consumer credit counseling service for low-fee guidance on how to clear up your debts and your record.

BUYING AFTER BANKRUPTCY

Dear Edith: My husband filed bankruptcy in July. We assumed a mortgage in the next January. Is it possible for us to get a mortgage through a bank? If so what is involved?—Mrs. T.E.

You will probably have to wait until two years after the discharge—not the filing—of the bankruptcy. Meanwhile, you were lucky to have enough cash for an assumable mortgage. Better stay put and count your blessings.

It will help your record if you pay the present mortgage on the very first day it's due. Nowadays some lenders are keeping track of whether payments are made at the beginning or end of the monthly grace period—even if no late payments are due. Every bit of evidence that you take your debts seriously is valuable in reestablishing your credit record.

NO INCOME VERIFICATION

Dear Edith: I am not employed, but would like to consider buying a home. I live with my boyfriend who could afford this but he cannot buy a house because of his bankruptcy. Would I be able to go through a mortgage plan I saw where the ad said "no income verification"?—R.E.

The ad may not have mentioned that you'd need at least a 25 percent down payment, but that's the usual requirement for low-documentation or no-documentation loans.

PAST CREDIT PROBLEMS

Dear Edith: My fiancee and I are planning to have a home built at a cost of $140,000. We want to put $80,000 down with $60,000 to be financed. My question: my fiancee filed for bankruptcy about five years ago. Second, I had three judgments against me in 1983, since paid. At present I have one charge account in good standing, and she has car payments. No other outstanding obligations.

I read or heard years ago about contract buying where a person could buy a home and have a certain amount of time to pay it off. Could you send me details?—Mr. W.A.

With your problems that far in the past, and your present good records, you should not have trouble borrowing on a regular mortgage. I assume, of course, that your income is capable of carrying the payments.

Most lending institutions will be impressed by your substantial down payment. A contract for deed (land contract) might not be appropriate for a new house.

EX-HUSBAND IS A VETERAN

Dear Edith: I would like to buy a house but I need to know if it is possible for me to obtain a VA mortgage based on my ex-husband's service. We have a 21-year-old son and it is his future I am thinking of.—Mrs. S.W.H.

I'm afraid VA loans are available only to

- the veteran, or
- veteran and current spouse, or
- surviving spouse of a veteran who died of a service-connected disability (if not remarried). Sorry.

QUALIFYING FOR VA LOAN

Dear Edith: My husband was in the U.S. Army from 1972 to 1975. Is he entitled to a VA loan?—Mrs. K.L.

If your husband had 180 days' active duty (or 90 days' during a war) and has a discharge that is "other than dishonorable," he may qualify for a VA loan. This assumes, of course, that he has acceptable credit and income, and hasn't used his entitlement previously. Even if he had, there are some ways to regain it.

For anyone enlisting after September 7, 1980, two full years' active service is required.

WHAT ABOUT ARMY RESERVE?

Dear Edith: I'm in the Army Reserve, have been there for 13 years. I have no active duty in the regular Army. I would like to know how I can go about buying my first house with their help. —Sgt. V.K.

No amount of time in the Reserve will qualify you for a VA mortgage. Sorry about that.

HOW MUCH DOWN FOR VA?

Dear Edith: My husband and I are in our early 60s. He has a certificate of eligiblity from the Veterans Administration with an entitlement of $27,500. How much down payment would we need for a house in the $90,000 range? Also can you tell us how much we would need for closing costs?—Mrs. B.P.

That certificate allows you to place a VA loan with nothing down, on any house you could afford to carry, up to a purchase price of $144,000. (Individual lenders may set varying top limits.) The VA recently raised its entitlement figure (amount of the government's guarantee) from $27,500 to $36,000.

Closing costs might run about $4,000 for a VA loan on a $90,000 house. Besides that, you'd need cash to prepay some property taxes and insurance.

THE VA RIDER

Dear Edith: I am enclosing something called a "VA Rider" that was on a purchase agreement I signed. From what I understand, the Veterans Administration requires this clause when a veteran buys a piece of property. I am not totally sure of this clause and wish you could explain how it affects the purchase agreement. —Mr. K.R.

That rider is required if the borrower wants to place a VA (or FHA) mortgage. It provides that if VA's appraiser doesn't find the place is worth the sale price, the buyer need not go through with the purchase and will receive back any earnest money deposit.

The buyer may, however, choose to go ahead and buy the place anyhow, with a lower VA mortgage than was requested, giving the seller the difference in cash. Or the seller may agree to a lower price.

VETERAN IS 71

Dear Edith: Is there any restriction on the age of an applicant for a VA mortgage? I am a veteran of WWII and am 71 years old. I have never used my veterans status to get a home loan. We are considering buying a condominium in Florida as a vacation home and would like to finance it through a VA loan. Our present home has no mortgage and is paid for. —Mr. K.N.K.

Your age won't enter into the mortgage application at all. In fact, human rights laws won't even let the lender ask or consider your age. And as you know, your VA loan entitlement never expires. Even if you'd used it before, you could regain all or part of it if the first house was sold and the mortgage was paid off or that first loan didn't use up your whole entitlement.

Your problems lie elsewhere. You will have to prove enough dependable income to handle monthly payments comfortably, just as any borrower does. Then again, not all condo developments meet standards for VA loans. Brokers in Florida should be able to direct you to those that do.

The one I just can't nail down is whether you can use your VA entitlement on a second home. One lender tells me it's acceptable if the property is suitable for year-round living and is not intended for rental use. Another says VA mortgages are meant only for a primary residence. Perhaps if you try several lenders you'll find one that interprets this point the way you'd like.

WOULDN'T TAKE VA BUYER

Dear Edith: When we bought our house three years ago, we wanted to use my GI loan, upon which the builder says he would not accept that as payment for the house. As we wanted the house we had to go to a bank for a conventional mortgage which we got.

Was there any law broken when the builder refused to accept my GI entitlement and if so have I any recourse? I cannot refinance my mortgage at this time, which is 10 percent. —K.B.

Some sellers refuse to accept offers in which the buyers state their intention to place VA (GI) mortgages, and as far as I know, they're within their rights. One reason might be that the VA won't let its veteran pay more than one point; if any more are required for the loan, the seller must pay them.

It seldom pays to refinance a mortgage unless you can drop your interest rate by at least 2 percent.

PRICE OF VA-MORTGAGED HOUSE

Dear Edith: Does the house have to cost less than $144K to use the VA loan benefit? —L.E.

If the particular lender agrees, a no-down-payment VA mortgage may be placed for as much as $144,000. You could pay more for the house, but anything above $144,000 would usually have to be in the form of a cash down payment.

USING VA IN CANADA

Dear Edith: I plan to build a home near Ottawa in Canada. Can I obtain a VA or FHA loan? I understand that some markets are opening up as a result of the Canadian free trade agreements.—Ms. N.N.L.

Good try, but no cigar. VA and FHA loans are placed through certain lending institutions in the United States, which lend on property located in their communities. The VA borrower must be a veteran, and the FHA borrower must be a permanent resident of the U.S.

VA ELIGIBILITY FOR $8,500

Dear Edith: I have a certificate of VA eligibility for $8,500. We want to buy a house priced, of course, much higher. Do you think the certificate will help toward at least part of a mortgage loan?—T.Y.

Currently the VA guarantees the top part of a mortgage loan, up to a maximum of $36,000. That guarantee would allow you to place a no-down-payment mortgage for as much as $144,000 (assuming, of course, that you could handle payments on such a high loan).

So I wonder why your certificate is for only $8,500. Did you use part of your VA entitlement in the past, on some other house you bought for your own residence? And is that loan still outstanding? Or do you have an old certificate, from the days when the VA guarantee was much lower?

In either case, write away for a new certificate. My guess is that you're entitled to a higher guarantee than $8,500, and it may be enough to let you place a nothing-down loan on the house you want.

CHAPTER 4

Real Estate Investment How-To's

"I heard this guy on cable TV..."

When I analyze reader letters about real estate investment, it looks as if most of them are triggered by too much watching of those get-rich-quick gurus on late-night cable TV. My responses make it clear what I think of them, and how I'd recommend starting out in investment.

Real estate investment is a fine goal for those who are prepared to put in some time studying, and some hard work locating, managing and marketing property. It's a solid way to get rich—but it's a matter of get-rich-slowly.

This collection begins with some miscellaneous letters, then moves to the TV-type queries. And, along the way, a question or two that was just too funny to publish.

SOMETHING ABOUT DEPRECIATION

Dear Edith: Could you please furnish me with some information about depreciation? I own a two-family income house, very old.—Mrs. C.C.

Depreciation is a bookkeeping fiction that allows you to charge as an "expense" a percentage of your cost for the property every year before you figure your taxable profit. The allowable percentage has varied over the years, depending on when the property was put into service as a rental.

Although depreciation isn't actually an expense, it can be deducted from your rental income along with genuine expenses. It often allows you to show a paper loss on the property for income tax purposes, even though you might have had some actual cash flow during the year.

RENTING OUT HALF

Dear Edith: If I buy a duplex with the idea of living in half and renting the other half, does the rented half qualify for depreciation expense on my income tax return? — Mr. A.A.

Yes.

BUY NOW FOR LATER

Dear Edith: On a recent trip South I visited many brokers with an eye to possibly purchasing a condo for retirement purposes, which I intend to do in several years. Several said "Buy now and let the federal government pay for it" and advised me to see my accountant with regard to this. Would you please explain what they meant? Would this be a tax write-off? — Mr. E.B.

Buying now and renting out for the next few years might give you certain amount of tax shelter for your other income — or might not.

Running the figures past an accountant is the best idea. Whether it's worth buying now depends on purchase price, probable rental income, estimated expenses (property tax, insurance, vacancies, maintenance, monthly fees, mortgage payments and cost of of hiring someone to oversee the unit while you're up north). The accountant would also consider your present income tax bracket before making a recommendation.

In general, your first real estate investment should be within half an hour of your home, where you can manage it yourself and keep an eye on it. I've received too many letters about resort property that didn't pan out and retirement plans that changed. I don't advise buying out of state unless you are ready to use the property yourself within a couple of years.

PUZZLED ABOUT DEPRECIATION

Dear Edith: Your answer to someone asking about a home office seemed to indicate that property that was depreciated really generated only a tax postponement. Do I understand this correctly? When analyzing rental property, for example, one should not figure in tax savings from depreciation? Because the depreciation amounts later will be taxed when the property is sold? — I.C.

I don't know if you've noticed, but where income tax is concerned, there is just about no free lunch. Yes, depreciation must be given back (recaptured) when income property is sold and the final tax bills come in. But investors and accountants feel that present tax savings usually outweigh possible increased liability in the indefinite future. More important, the investor gets the use of the saved money along the way.

There are two ways depreciation might never be recaptured. When a home office is involved, things can sometimes work out so that past depreciation doesn't matter. If the space is later returned to residential use, a lower cost basis may not hurt the taxpayer who uses one of the special home-sellers' tax breaks to shield profit from federal income tax.

And the person who inherits depreciated property takes it with a new stepped-up cost basis, at current value—death as the ultimate tax shelter.

INVESTOR'S DOWN PAYMENT

Dear Edith: Could you please indicate from your experience the best source of financing for a real estate investor? Is there any way to obtain financing without the usual 15 to 20 percent down?—Mr. S.N.

There isn't any one best way to finance real estate. So many various mortgage plans are out there because each arrangement fits certain borrowers' needs better than others.

When you talk of "the usual 15 to 20 percent down," you must be referring to bank loans offered to investors. For those buying their own homes, many mortgages are available with lower down payments.

For an investor, the usual source for financing with little or nothing down is directly from the seller.

IN MILITARY, GOING OVERSEAS

Dear Edith: I am in the military and due to transfer overseas in June. I have been offered a property with two houses on it for $75,000. Each rents for $300 a week. Do you think I can raise the rent? Can I select new tenants? What are my responsiblities as a landlord? I can use some advice.—R.W.

Yes you can, and my advice is—forget it.

Rental property requires on-the-spot attention. Weekly rentals often mean transient tenants and lots of maintenance, and you couldn't possibly keep track of things from abroad.

FINDING INCOME PROPERTY

Dear Edith: I am 25 years old, have a steady job of eight years and a good credit history. But cannot afford a home in the area where I'd like to live. I am very happy where I live now and have low rent.

But I would like to invest in a home to build some kind of equity. Would it be a mistake to buy a duplex or multi-family for a first house and not live in it? And is it really possible to get into something with a positive cash flow or at least break-even?—S.H.

If you think you have the temperament to be a landlord and if you're willing to put in some work, buying a duplex or multi-family is an excellent way for a young person to start out in real estate.

Yes, there are opportunities for property that will carry itself or even produce a small cash flow. You just need the right broker and a good accountant to help you identify them.

TAKEN OUT AND SHOT

Dear Edith: I am interested in buying property and over-financing it by getting a loan for 80 percent of its value and having the seller carry back the balance plus enough for me to get some money left over from the proceeds of the loan (thus over-financing).

But I have a major problem of being under 18 so I cannot take title to property or be held accountable for debts. Is there a way of deferring the property to someone else for one year? How could I go about making money now by over-financing these properties?—Mr. B.A.

It's clear you've been watching late-night TV.

Over-financing, or any financing for that matter, isn't a way to make money. It's a way to borrow money. The difference is an important one; borrowed money must be paid back. Whoever got you all excited about over-financing ought to be taken out and shot.

The "creative" techniques you speak of are dangerous. Many of them involve lying to lenders about what other debts you're placing against the property. You could search for years to find a seller willing enter into the transaction you describe. And have you thought about the problem of collecting enough rental income to pay for those loans you want to pile up?

No matter what the hot-shot investment seminars teach, there is no easy way to make money without working. Managing property is time-consuming. You must learn how to judge people, handle tenants, inspect property, analyze income and expenses, make small repairs—and that's just for starters.

Real estate is a terrific investment. To prepare yourself, spend the time until you are 18 taking evening courses at local schools or colleges, reading and studying. Line up a lawyer and accountant, who will be vital to your success.

TEMPTING TAX SALES

Dear Edith: How do you purchase property on county tax sale? Is this a good or risky business of acquiring real estate? In the papers you see whole pages of property for sale of back taxes.—Mrs. O.L.

Don't get too excited about those lists in the paper. Often they are just notices that current taxes are being placed as a legal claim (lien) against various properties.

Even when real estate is sold for unpaid taxes, it usually brings more than the tax bill due. An auction is held in an attempt to sell the parcel for full market value. Bidders must be prepared to pay cash.

Sometimes one can find a bargain that way, but the process takes a certain amount of financial sophistication. The purchaser should have the protection of a lawyer's assistance along the way.

BEAUTIFUL TWO-YEAR-OLD

Dear Edith: Back in 1986 I claimed bankruptcy and am currently reestablishing credit with my credit union. I make $30,000 a year and pay $260 a month in child support. I do not own any property or have a lot of money in the bank. I am very interested in investing in real estate hopefully with no money down but am very curious to see what you could offer me.

I have a little girl who is two years old and beautiful and would love to make her future very very bright. —Mr. K.N.

Your last sentence sounds uncomfortably like the upbeat testimonials one hears on those cable TV programs, and makes me nervous. Success in real estate takes hard work, and will be particularly challenging if you try to do it with no cash and a recent bankruptcy. Motivation and a hopeful outlook are fine, but you still must put in time, study and effort.

Start by signing up for a course in basic real estate at a local school or college—the kind of course beginning salespersons take. That will give you background and a vocabulary, you'll meet others who are interested in real estate, and you should come out with some idea of what to do next. If you really mean what you say, that's the place to begin your hard work. If it seems like too much effort, perhaps you're just indulging in wishful thinking.

BUYING FROM AN ESTATE

Dear Edith: I am interested in purchasing real estate during estate settlements. How do I go about doing this? —K.H.

Beats me. I don't know of any special techniques for locating such property.

Sometimes a family member takes over the deceased's real estate, sometimes the executor or an heir puts it on the market.

You might find a real estate broker who would search the multiple listings for property listed by "Estate of...." And I suppose you could follow up obituaries and call survivors asking if they have a house to sell, but that does seem a bit crass.

BARGAINS FROM THE GOVERNMENT

Dear Edith: I received this letter in the mail telling me that I can buy a house dirt cheap from the government sales. Is this really possible or is it just someone who is trying to make a quick profit on my ignorance? I had to sell my house in a divorce several years ago. I was left with a lot of bills and I can't seem to save enough to buy another home.

Does this dirt cheap thing work? Otherwise I know I will never be able to afford a house where I really want to live.—Ms. F.

Thank you for including the material that came to you in the mail. I've read all five pages carefully. They keep saying you can make up to $10,000 a month buying government-seized property and reselling it. Nowhere is there any mention of the fact that if you could find such property, you'd have to buy for cash.

Yes, there are government-foreclosed houses for sale through the FHA and VA. Some are available to the highest bidder for all cash. With others, you must qualify for a mortgage in the normal way: some cash, good credit, dependable income and not too many other debts.

Lists of VA and FHA foreclosed homes are published regularly in the newspapers. Bids are placed through local real estate brokers, and most agents can help you with the paper-work needed to bid on them.

Don't send money out of town for any guide on how to do it. I'm afraid there's no magic formula to help you.

COMMENT ON NOTHING DOWN

Dear Edith: Please comment on the feasibility of the practices taught in the no-money-down or similar courses. Legally the ideas are sound but how applicable are they in real life?—Mr. N.O.

The advice in no-money-down courses and tapes works—sometimes. It depends on willingness of the would-be investor to do some hard work, and depends even more on the state of the real estate market, which varies widely from one area to another and from one time to another.

Certain of the courses are good, others skate on thin ice from a legal or moral point of view. You can do as well, and for less expense, with a good book. I was very much impressed, recently, with *Successful Real Estate Investing* by Peter Miller (Harper and Row).

TAKING A $4,500 COURSE

Dear Edith: I would appreciate your opinion on a real estate investing course I am seriously considering. It is being taught by a well-known investor. He *and his associates will crash course educate people (me) for $5,000. It is a one-week course with actual property purchasing done. Then consultants will be available after the course for support and guidance.*

The course is guaranteed to at least triple your seminar costs in the first year or your money back (if you meet the minimal requirements). I would love to learn about investing and making money. Working hard is no problem for me, if there's gold at the end of the rainbow. What do you think? — Mr. E.U.G.

I think $5,000 is an unnecessary sum to pay for the education you want. I double-checked with one of the best investment brokers I know, who has argued in the past that some of those seminars can be a good way to learn a great deal quickly. But when he heard the price of admission, he just laughed and agreed with me.

The man you mention has sound ideas; they might or might not work in your area, depending on how much effort, study and time you want to put in. For only a few dollars, though, you can go to a bookstore, buy Robert Allen's best-seller *Nothing Down* (Simon and Schuster) and get most of the same information.

After you've worked your way through the book, you'll be in a better position to judge how you want to start out in investment.

About that triple-your-money-back guarantee: I'd be interested in hearing what those minimum requirements might be. It'd also be helpful to hear from investors who may have taken such a course — did they actually go on to use what they learned, and was the money well spent?

LETTER I DIDN'T PRINT

Dear Edith: I want to know how to calculate if its worth to me to buy a house. My desire is to buy 100 single houses. Right now I don't know how to do it. Please advice. Respectfully...

CHAPTER 5

Landlord and Tenant

"I have this pesky tenant...I have this rotten landlady."

Mostly it's landlords who write in. Tenants' questions come down to one major complaint: how to get the security deposit back. For that one I often recommend small claims court, unless the community has a special agency to deal with such problems.

It's hard to know what to say when I hear from someone who's obviously not cut out to be a landlord. "My tenant won't give me a key—what advice can you give?" And sometimes it's best not to stir things up further.

LETTERS I DIDN'T PRINT

Dear Edith: I have a problem with my tenant. I rented a five room house to him. I have so much trouble with him. He's a collector, he makes money, brings the garbage on my land and makes a terrible looking garbage pile, it's a very bad sight. I have asked him so many times to clean it up but he makes a joke out of it. I guess because I'm a widow he takes advantage of me. I only charge him 70 dollars a month no utilities included.... I asked him to move. I don't want no more renters. He tells me he'll take 90 days if he goes.... If I go to an attorney it's hard for me and I know they're expensive. Please tell me what I can do. Do not put my name in the paper or he'll give me more trouble.—Mrs. R.J.

So I didn't.

Sometimes you wonder what's the story behind the letter, as in this next one.

Dear Edith: I have deed to a three-unit apartment... am looking in same area and need all the information I can get on using the apartment for a blanket loan... believe it or not I am a good landlord thanks to the district justice in my area. I did take my lumps and all is well now.... Please help me understand how I could use my apartment to purchase another and not support everyone else, bankers, real estate people etc. — Mr. L.S.

Don't you just wonder what kind of lumps that district justice handed out — and why?

NEW LANDLORD AND LEASES

Dear Edith: I have just purchased a double house and will be living in one half. Could you please advise me as to developing a lease for tenants? I know pre-made forms are available but I would like to know what common clauses can be deleted or should be added to protect my investment. Yes, I know I'm new to this but I hope to avoid common mistakes. — Mr. C.C.

Careful tenant selection is at least as important as what's in a lease. After you've been at it a while you learn that what you're legally entitled to and what you can get as a practical matter are two different things. What use is it if tenants owe you such-and-such funds when they don't have the money to pay?

Learn to judge potential tenants by whether they

- Pay their bills on time (ask for a credit report)
- Have stable employment (again, ask)
- Will spend no more than a quarter of their income on your rent (otherwise, they'll be overextended)
- Keep their car neat and their kids under control
- Have enough cash on hand to pay your security deposit and first month's rent in advance.

It's better to lose rent while waiting for the right tenants than to lock yourself into a problem situation.

As for the lease: the new investor's most common mistake is trying to do without an accountant and a lawyer. The attorney is the person to help with your lease. Remember, though, that a lease is only a piece of paper. What's more important is the intention of the two parties to treat each other fairly.

GETTING A CREDIT REPORT

Dear Edith: In judging potential tenants, you wrote "See if they pay their bills on time (ask for a credit report)."

Who do you ask? Is the tenant to request a report from the credit bureau? Should we as landlords offer to pay the fee? Our lawyer says to acquire a report we would have to join a bureau at a cost of thousands of dollars. Hardly worth it for the one duplex we own. But we have been stung more than once in judging people and can't afford many more losses. —Mrs. K.N.

You needn't pay for a report on everyone who wants to rent your duplex. Prospective tenants can go to a credit bureau and obtain a report themselves, for a small fee. While there, they can talk with counselors about how to clear up any inaccuracies or problems that appear.

Tell your lawyer, by the way, that membership in a credit bureau is nowhere as expensive as he thinks.

BIG LOSS ON TENANTS

Dear Edith: I took my tenant to court for non-payment of rent, but they moved out of town and it took time till I could take possession of the vacant house through eviction proceedings. The whole thing has cost me legal fees of $2,000, and there will be another fee of $1,000 plus 25 percent of whatever is collected, if I decide to hire them to collect the judgment for me.

This has stunned me. The resulting financial burden has been tremendous, adding up to $8,640 including lost rent. I do know their current address, car plate number, and bank accounts but the banks won't impart information. I am writing to seek your advice on how to go about recouping some of this amount and where to get free legal assistance in this matter. —Ms. D.D.

There's no free legal help for someone in your situation. You've had a tough one, but that's part of the landlord business. Next time you'll run a credit check on prospective tenants and jump on them the first time rent payments are even a few days late.

Turn the judgments over to the legal firm's collection department, so you may recover at least some of the loss.

LANDLORD'S DEDUCTIBLE EXPENSES

Dear Edith: Do you know about tax breaks or deductions for an individual who owns a home, moves to another state and rents his present home? I mean things like is there any deductible for travel to manage the house, roof repairs etc.? —Ms. O.V.

If you keep your present home and rent it out, you have become a real estate investor, and one of the first things you need is a professional to advise you.

An accountant can guide you in the matter of travel expense, for which there is no simple answer. Repairs are a deductible expense for a landlord.

Better think the whole thing over first. Being an absentee landlord is difficult. What will happen when the roof springs a leak? Who will track down tenants if they get behind on the rent and have an unlisted phone? In general, your first real estate investment should be within an hour's driving distance of your home; half an hour is better.

NO KEY TO THE APARTMENT

Dear Edith: My tenant has violated her lease several times. Also I do not have a key for the apartment. How do I go about it? Or what can I do?—N.K.

You are entitled to keep a key for the tenant's apartment, though you cannot enter except in an emergency or by prior arrangement.

As for how to get the key and how to get the tenant to live up to her lease—that's a matter of personalities. Perhaps you weren't meant to be a landlord. Tenant selection is a skill; so is asserting your rights.

You don't say what the violations of lease were. If you or neighbors are disturbed, by loud noise for example, ask the police to handle it. If the problem is late rent payments and you want to reclaim the apartment, have a lawyer step in.

RETURN ON INVESTMENT

Dear Edith: I have a newer 3-bedroom ranch, 2 bathroom, 2-car garage, 1,200 square foot ranch with no basement. The house is worth $105,000. My payments are $964 monthly. I am trying to decide what rent to charge. What type of return on investment should a person get on rental property?—Mr. S.Y.

You're going at the problem backwards.

You can't set the rent figure by the return you'd like to get. In the end, rents are really set by tenants. Your place will bring in whatever someone is willing to pay to live in it—and that's someone who is comparing it with everything else up for rent in that neighborhood.

FAMILIES WITH CHILDREN

Dear Edith: Some time ago I read about a law that came into effect in 1989 that forbids discrimination in housing because of age or children. I interpreted it to mean that unless an adult community can prove that they are strictly senior citizens (over 65) they are not going to be able to restrict younger people with or without children to come in and purchase houses.

Do you have any information on this new law? I am a senior citizen living in an adult community. —N.W.

The new federal law, which prohibits housing discrimination against families with children, went into effect March 13, 1989. Adult-only communities can retain their restrictions if they have significant facilities and services specifically designed to meet the physical or social needs of the elderly and all of their units are occupied by persons 62 or older, or 80 percent of occupants are at least 55. Those presently in such communities who do not meet the age standards were not counted in the initial calculation and were not required to move out.

Also protected by the new federal regulations are would-be buyers or tenants with physical and mental handicaps. Federal law also prohibits discrimination based on race, sex, national origin and religion. Some states add other protected classes—source of income, political affiliation, marital status and age, for example.

Most laws provide some exceptions, typically for rental of rooms or an apartment in one's own home. Where race is concerned, however, no exceptions apply.

CAN LANDLORD ENTER?

Dear Edith: If I have a tenant three months behind in rent, I am holding a rubber check, does the landlord have the right to enter apartment with keys when tenant is in or out, for any reason?—Mr. K.S.

You're mixing up two different matters. As a landlord you have certain legal remedies, but until the tenant has been evicted he or she still has the right to privacy. The overdue rent and bounced check don't change the fact that you may enter only with permission or in an emergency.

TENANT SUBLET THE HOUSE

Dear Edith: I rented a house to a man who moved out, didn't notify me. Then he rented it to other people charging more than he was paying. He continued to pay me rent so I wouldn't be wise to what he was doing. The other people moved out. Although I kept the security deposit it won't near cover the damage they did. Can I take him to small claims court? He is a working man. —Mrs. C.S.

Small claims court is ideal for a situation like yours. You can do it yourself at little cost, without a lawyer, and tell your story to a judge. The original tenant is probably responsible for that damage, particularly since he never asked your approval of his subtenants.

RENTING IN FLORIDA

Dear Edith: In attempting to rent an apartment we have been told that Florida law provides that a condominium cannot be rented for less than three months. Is there such a law? —Mr. E.K.C.

No, but a particular condominium development—or a whole community—could have such a binding regulation, aimed at discouraging occupancy by transient renters.

FORCED TO SIGN

Dear Edith: I live in an apartment complex in which I signed a two-year lease. In addition, I was forced to sign a land-tax agreement with my landlord.

I just received a letter to the effect that taxes went up and I will have to pay an additional $5 a month. Can I deduct this on my income tax return? —V.E.

I'm not sure what your land-tax agreement was, but if it said the landlord could pass on to you any increase in property taxes, I'm afraid you're still just paying nondeductible rent. Your landlord gets to claim claim property taxes as an expense against rental income.

WRITING A LEASE-OPTION

Dear Edith: I rent a summer home by the year and would like to make improvements but don't want to lose the money I'd be putting in to someone else's property. The owner is a little hesitant about selling at this time.

I've heard of a lease with purchase agreement. How does this work and from whom do I obtain the right documents? —Mr. K.G.M.

If you want a lease-option, your first job is to get the owner to agree that you can buy in the future if you choose. The two of you must then decide how much rent you'll pay, and for how long you'd have the right to buy the place at a stated price. Then you take the terms to your lawyer, who draws up a legally binding contract you can both sign.

The seller would probably want his own lawyer's input also, to make sure both of you have your interests protected.

LANDLORD'S EVICTION TECHNIQUE

Dear Edith: You advised Mrs. C.S. to talk with a lawyer as the first step to evicting a tenant. A friend of mine who owns rental property described to me his second-to-last resort tactic.

He would make an offer like "If you're out by Friday, I'll give you $300. If not, I'll evict you." The tenant may be tempted to leave. The landlord frees his property for immediate lease to paying tenants and avoids legal expenses and lengthy ugly eviction proceedings.

What are your thoughts on this technique?—P.O.

It's interesting, and might be effective in some situations.

My "see a lawyer" advice brought mail from many readers who pointed out that one can institute eviction on one's own without a lawyer (in some communities with particularly simple, prompt procedures).

But the particular landlady who originally asked my advice—after her tenants were five months behind in rent—clearly wasn't equipped to be a successful do-it-yourselfer.

RENT IN ADVANCE

Dear Edith: My son and seven friends (all seniors) are going to lease a house for the college year, two semesters, starting in September. They have already each paid a $100 deposit. The landlady says they each have to pay $750 by August 1—one semester's rent apiece.

This does not seem fair. The landlady will have $6,000 to use over during August while my son and his friends are losing interest on their money. She says they won't have access until September. Is what she's doing legal?—N.R.

Unless that community has some unusual rent regulations, it's legal all right. Owning a house means you get to say who lives in it. If your son and his friends don't like the terms, they needn't go ahead with the deal.

Putting up all the money now does seem a bit much, but the landlady will probably be turning down other prospective tenants over the summer. In a group of eight average college students, she may fear at least one will change plans, drop out of school, quarrel or want to move in with someone else.

I'll bet the college asks a whole semester's rent in advance for its dormitories.

ADDRESSES INDEFINITE

Dear Edith: I own a house jointly with my brother. We are considering renting the home and as both our addresses will be indefinite for a period we question where the renter will make monthly payments? Do banks perform this service or possibly an accounting firm? How about endorsement of the checks if they are made out to us?

Also, would you suggest trying to rent on our own or going through a broker? First time around is a learning experience. —Mr. L.E.

It's easy to see you haven't had experience as landlords, if you think the owner's main duty is collecting rent.

Tenant selection calls for skill, and you should have a broker's help. Then, what happens while you are off at your indefinite addresses and the water heater bursts in the middle of the night? When your tenant is transferred out of town and needs to break the lease?

Someone will have to be on the spot, with authority to handle problems. Not many real estate firms will take on the management of a single house, but find one that will. Be prepared to pay a percentage of the rent for the service. By the time you've done that, it's likely you won't have much of a cash flow—or any, depending on your mortgage situation.

HOLDOVER TENANT SKIPPED

Dear Edith: Could you explain what a holdover tenant is? Our tenant stays over after a two-year lease expires. Pays rent for the holdover month. Moves out on the fifth of the following month and offers to pay 5/30 of the rent for that month. Aren't we entitled to a full month's rental plus 30 days' notice? Your opinion, please. —Mr. B.S.

I think you are entitled to a full month's rental and one month's notice (in some states, two months' notice) from the date the rent is due. It would be more useful, however to seek the opinion of a judge. Small claims court would be appropriate.

BAD SITUATION WITH LANDLADY

Dear Edith: I am in a bad situation with my landlady. I signed a lease and moved in at a cost of $500. Then I found I have neither heat nor hot water. I complained to my landlady. She brought a plumber, and found it is very expensive for her to furnish hot water on my floor.

She is telling me to move out. I do not have another $500 to move. I am enclosing my lease. Please help me. —Mr. N.K.

I don't need to read your lease. Any landlord, lease or not, makes what is known as an "implied warrant of habitability," guaranteeing that the rented unit is fit to live in. Heat and hot water would be included in minimum standards.

Call city hall and ask for the department that handles tenants' complaints.

PART 2

Home Owning

"My mortgage payment went down. Don't I have any rights?"

Most monthly mortgage payments include PITI, the initials standing for principal, interest, taxes and insurance. The first two items take care of the debt, the last two involve the escrow, or trust, account the lender establishes to make sure those bills are paid on time. And plenty of readers don't understand what's going on—can't blame them when it's such a complicated matter. Some letters I don't like to use in the paper—why make fun of people?

CHAPTER 6

Home Owning—Mortgages

LETTERS I DIDN'T PRINT

Dear Ms. Lank: I read where VA loans interest decreased in your column. Please send details on when this happened and how I go about notifying my bank. I read this somewhere before and received no cooperation from my bank at that time. Thanks.

You can hear the righteous indignation there. That's someone who undoubtedly has a fixed-interest loan and doesn't realize that the new rates apply only to new mortgages.

To Whom It Concern: We bought a house two years ago and the end of last year our monthly mortgage went down. Could you explain how this could affect a person in the long run? Do I have any rights, can I change this if I want to? There is a name for this but I forgot what it is called. Thank you.

That's the only letter I ever received complaining about a mortgage payment that was too small. It could be an adjustable rate mortgage. Or possibly the escrow account contained an overage, so payments will be lower for a while.

Dear Edith: We would like to pay the mortgage off by paying extra every month along with the regular payment. Is this a wise move? If so, which will be the best, paying extra on principal, interest or escrow? Thank you.

No, I don't have to make them up. The answer is, of course, that only principal payments go to reduce the debt. What do you suppose they think escrow is?

NOT PAID DOWN ENOUGH

Dear Edith: My mother purchased a house back in 1971 for $20,000. Here is the problem: since then her mortgage company has changed hands four *or five times. Now her mortgage balance is still somewhere around $15,000 and this is with monthly payments of $250. This is absolutely ridiculous: the property should be nearly paid for!*

I have a feeling someone's getting rich off my Mom. Where would we begin to investigate to determine if we have been taken for a ride? My Mom is a senior citizen on a fixed income so attorney fees would be difficult but is that the only alternative?—Sign me very very concerned, Ms. D.N.C.

Don't see a lawyer. Your mother's mortgage is right on schedule. It looks as if she took out a 30-year loan. At this point, 75 percent still due is about right.

You're forgetting about interest. At the beginning, most of your mother's monthly payment went for interest on the debt, with only a small amount left each month to reduce the principal owed. At the start she paid interest on $20,000. By now she owes interest on only $15,000.

She should be half paid off in approximately year 23 (1994). Then for the last seven years, as less and less interest is due, the debt is reduced swiftly, and by 2001 she will owe nothing. That was the original plan, and it's working out properly.

ABOUT EQUITY ACCELERATION

Dear Edith: Could you please give me some information on equity acceleration, as I would like to pay off my mortgage as soon as possible.—Ms. G.T.

Putting extra money into paying off your loan extra quickly may or may not be a good idea, depending on your total financial situation.

If money burns a hole in your pocket, you could be wise to sock it away where you can't get at it; extra payments are a sort of enforced savings. If you expect to send a child to college in a few years, or to retire, clearing the debt as soon as possible may be just right. The same holds true if your mortgage is at a high rate of interest.

But once you have sent off the extra money, you can't tap it easily. Taking out an equity line of credit in the future, or a second mortgage, may involve closing costs and a higher rate of interest. (In Texas, it isn't possible at all.) And it makes no sense to send extra money in on the mortgage at the same time you are borrowing on a credit card or car loan. Mortgage interest is usually deductible.

If you do want to accelerate your payments, discuss the recommended procedure with your lending institution. You need to make sure the additional money is credited properly.

DOESN'T COME OUT RIGHT

Dear Edith: My bank told me $20 of my payment goes to principal, to reduce the amount I owe them. But when I multiplied $20 by the number of payments remaining, it doesn't come out right. According to what I figure, we'd have to pay an additional 60 payments, which would be 5 years, before the debt was paid off. I haven't said anything to the bank yet about this. Should I see an attorney? Or am I not figuring it out right?—F.I.

Relax, be happy, don't worry.

Your principal payment, the part that reduces the remaining debt, would be at $20 for only one specific month. The following month, you'd be borrowing $20 less, so you'd owe a bit less interest. That would leave a little more of your payment to go toward principal, and you'd pay off, for example, $20.35 that next month. Then you'd be borrowing $20.35 less for the third month, so you'd owe even less interest and might have $20.71 to apply toward principal.

My figures are random examples, of course, but that's the way you'll pay off your mortgage according to schedule.

LOWER IN OFF-MONTHS

Dear Edith: My husband is self-employed in seasonal service work, and the business is growing nicely, though, as I say, it's only seasonal. Can mortgage payments be adjusted so as to be higher during the busy months of April through October when money is more available and lower payments during the off-months?—Mrs. E.K.

Not possible. Make your own adjustments by setting aside extra funds in the good months, to be used over the winter.

THAT APR MYSTERY

Dear Edith: Although my mortgage is at 13.5 percent, the closing notice we got says annual percentage rate 14.96 percent. Confusing!—Mr. S.E.

If you took out a loan at 13.5 percent and paid several points in up-front interest, you'd really be paying more than 13.5 percent. How much more? The answer depends on how many years the loan is likely to run, among other factors. The lending institution must let you know exactly what it works out to, and that figure is known as the annual percentage rate (APR).

The APR is a useful tool for comparing one mortgage plan with another, when points and financing charges become so complicated you can't see which would be better.

DROPPING PMI CHARGES

Dear Edith: I just read that some home owners can stop paying PMI, private mortgage insurance, when their equity rises to 25 percent or more because of higher market value. We purchased our house five years ago and we may be getting close to that 25 percent equity because it has gone up in value. Can you elaborate on this? — Mr. T.C.

In order to convince your lender that you owe less than 75 percent of the house's present value, you'll need to furnish a new appraisal — some lenders say they want two appraisal reports. The cost of appraisal will be more than you could expect to save by dropping the private mortgage insurance, so there's the catch. It's almost never worth the expense.

On the other hand, when your debt drops to less than 75 percent (some mortgages stipulate 70 percent) of original purchase price, you do have a good case for ending PMI premiums. Most lenders say they'll take care of it automatically when you reach that point, but I'd keep track and follow up myself.

CHECKING THE BANK'S FIGURES

Dear Edith: When the bank adjusts my interest rate on November 1, my papers say the interest rate will be calculated by adding two percentage points to an index. The index is "the weekly average yield on United States Treasury Securities adjusted to a constant maturity of one year as made available by the Federal Reserve Board." Where do I find the index value as of that date so that I can calculate and check the bank's figures? — Mr. H.S.

The figure you want is published in the business section of many newspapers. Look for "One-year T-bills."

Banks have been known to make mistakes, and you are wise to plan on checking the interest rate adjustment yourself.

BIWEEKLY MORTGAGE

Dear Edith: Recently I was offered a plan to pay off our 30-year mortgage in 20 years by paying our loan installments every two weeks instead of each month. Is this a good idea? Or is it just a scheme to make money for them? — Mrs. C.I.

Of course lending institutions make money through mortgage loans; that's their business and you can't fault them for it.

Most biweekly plans require automatic withdrawal from your bank account; this may or may not suit your budget. There is nothing wrong with the plan if it feels right for you.

WHAT'S FHA INSURANCE FOR?

Dear Edith: Regarding FHA-insured loans, can you tell me what the insurance is for, and the mortgagor's liability after the property is sold and mortgage assumed?—E.W.

FHA insurance, paid for by the borrower (mortgagor), protects the lending institution against loss if the property is seized for nonpayment and can't be sold for enough to cover the debt and legal costs. Even though the lender would be reimbursed, the borrower is still personally responsible for any shortfall.

Because the last owner is the one who had financial difficulty, the original borrower could be the one required to make up the loss. It is wise, therefore, to check the financial health of a buyer who proposes to take over one's FHA loan along with the house.

The original borrower is always personally responsible unless a "formal assumption" process is used, under which the new borrower proves satisfactory credit and income to the lending institution.

Even with nonformal assumption, most FHA mortgages placed after December 1, 1986, require anyone assuming the loan to prove financial ability to the lender's satisfaction. For many of those loans, the original borrower will be released from liability five years after an assumption.

MORTGAGE INSURANCE OR LIFE INSURANCE?

Dear Edith: You said that people with a VA mortgage didn't pay for insurance. I had a VA mortgage and we always thought that we were paying insurance that was included in our house payment.—Mr. S.C.

If you had a VA (GI) mortgage, you weren't paying any mortgage insurance premium. You might have been buying mortgage *life* insurance, which is a different matter.

The borrower on an FHA mortgage, on the other hand, does pay for mortgage insurance. This has nothing to do with life insurance, or with death—it protects the lender in case of foreclosure.

ABOUT MORTGAGE INSURANCE

Dear Edith: My father died in 1974 and yet the bank has not stopped the payments on a home loan insured by the bank. Where do I write in Washington about this?—E.N.S.

The term "mortgage insurance" is commonly used for two different things. One type protects the lending institution against loss. It takes the form of FHA insurance or private mortgage insurance (PMI). It doesn't involve any death benefits.

Mortgage life insurance, on the other hand, is a form of decreasing term insurance that does pay off the remaining mortgage balance upon the borrower's death.

Look through any papers you may have pertaining to your father's loan. Study the year-end statements the lending institution should presently furnish. Ignore charges for FHA or PMI. If you find references to mortgage life insurance, take all your papers to a lawyer for consultation.

If you want to contact authorities, forget Washington and try the state banking department.

RAISING ESCROW PAYMENTS

Dear Edith: It seems that every time I get involved with a mortgage company, they raise the escrow payments without justification. What is the best way to handle this practice?—Mr. E.H.

Do you understand the use of the escrow account—to pay your next property tax bills and home-owners' insurance premiums? Your lender should be able to justify the charges by estimating what those future payments will amount to. Most of us take for granted that such charges will go up each year.

Discuss the matter with your mortgage servicing department, and if you are still not convinced the raises are justified, contact the state banking department.

UNHAPPY WITH SECONDARY MARKET

Dear Edith: I don't understand mortgage selling. My original mortgage holder sold my mortgage. I felt more secure when a bank held the mortgage because it seemed "legitimate." Is there any danger that those changes could cause me to lose my house? Could the costs increase? Why do they do that? Why doesn't the borrower have a choice?—Ms. N.F.S.

In the old days, banks lent out their depositors' savings, then made more loans as they collected the money month by month over a period of years. You would have been comfortable with that system, keeping your relationship with the original local lender.

Nowadays, though, most mortgages are resold as yours was. Your bank put together a package of loans and sold to a large investor in what is known as the secondary market.

So now you must deal with out-of-towners. Doing so may irritate you, but there's no particular danger. All the terms of your loan remain the same.

The community benefits, because your bank promptly regained the money it lent out, and can turn right around and make more mortgage loans in the local area.

THREATENED VA FORECLOSURE

Dear Edith: Can the bank which holds my VA mortgage threaten to foreclose when I'm late with just one payment?—Mr. G.Y.

On a VA loan, the bank can't foreclose after just one late or missed payment. It can, however, write a letter pointing out that you will be in danger of losing your home if you didn't meet your promised obligations on time.

CHAPTER 7

Home Owning and the IRS

"So can I deduct the points or not?"

What's the difference between death and taxes? Death doesn't change every time Congress meets.

Well, it's not quite that bad. But the alert real estate owner must monitor shifting regulations on deductibility of closing costs, mortgage interest and property taxes. Investors have seen abrupt changes, in recent years, in the length of time for that delightful tax break known as depreciation—at its most generous, 18 years, at its most stingy, more than 31 years.

MORE ABOUT POINTS

Dear Edith: Hi! What are points?—Mr. V.S.C.

Each point is one percent of a new mortgage being placed. It represents extra interest on the loan, in a one-time lump sum at the beginning. On a $50,000 loan, three points would be $1,500. They can be paid by the borrower, or in some cases by the seller of the property, depending on what was agreed in the purchase contract.

Points paid by a seller are not income-tax-deductible, because they are not paid on his or her own loan. The buyer's points are deductible in the year they're paid, if the property is one's own home. For income property, or refinancing, points can be deducted, but only bit by bit over a period of years.

POINTS STILL NOT DEDUCTIBLE

Dear Edith: You have stated that the points a seller pays are not deductible. Here is a specific case: I have sold my house to a couple who are applying for a VA mortgage. I was told by my real estate agent that I must pay all but one of the buyers' points (VA regulation?). This forces me to pay five points. Are these points tax-deductible for me?—T.Y.

Points are deductible when they are prepaid interest on one's own loan, but you cannot deduct interest you pay on someone else's debt. This applies even when you have no choice in the matter, as with a VA loan.

Points are one of your costs of selling, and they reduce taxable profit. This can be of some value if you're selling income property.

WHAT TO DEDUCT

Dear Edith: I bought property in the last quarter of 1988 and here are some of the "Closing Costs" on my statement: fire insurance, credit report, appraisal, survey, legal, title insurance, loan origination fee, discount fees (points), recording fees, real estate property taxes. Which of the above heads of expenditure can I use as a deduction on my 1988 income tax return?—Mr. L.S.

You can consider only those things you paid for yourself; forget anything paid by the seller. If that's your own home, you can deduct the property taxes and the discount fee.

If it's income property, you need professional help with your tax return. Property taxes are immediately deductible, and fire insurance is also a current expense (not exactly a deduction). Most of the rest can be charged off for income property, but only bit by bit over a period of years; you'd need an accountant to sort things out.

NEW RULES ON INTEREST

Dear Edith: Our house is pretty well paid for. Before mortgage rates get any higher, we want to refinance our home and put the extra money away for our daughter's college. She won't start until a year from September. Will there be any problem with deducting the interest we pay? It is for an educational purpose, but not right away.—Mr. N.M.

There's no problem at all. That awkward "only for medical or educational expenses" rule has been scrapped; it only applied for one year.

You can deduct mortgage interest on up to a total of one million dollars' borrowing for purchase or improvement of a home (or even two homes—residence plus vacation property). In addition, you can deduct interest on up to $100,000 additional "home equity" borrowing. No restrictions on how the loan is used.

For most of us, that should pretty much cover the whole thing.

DEDUCTING FOR LOAN

Dear Edith: I keep seeing a lot about interest on new mortgages, if the loan is greater than the original cost of the home. My son, would he have a problem or can he deduct the interest on a mortgage if he got one now? It would be on the house I gave him and my original price would be lower than the mortgage he got.—Mr. T.C.

Your son did take over your cost basis for the property. His basis includes also money spent by either of you for permanent improvements over the years.

Beyond cost basis, your son can take an income tax deduction for interest on an additional $100,000 borrowed against the house, no matter what the money is used for.

CREDIT UNION RULES

Dear Edith: My credit union told me that if I borrow money for a condo it could not call it a home loan, but it would be a personal loan. Does this mean I could not use the interest on it for a federal income tax deduction?—S.A.

It doesn't matter so much what the credit union calls the loan. The important point is whether it takes a lien (financial claim) against the condo in return for the money. If the real estate is not pledged for the debt, you would indeed have a personal loan.

Interest on personal loans may be deductible in some states, but tax reform phased it out on your federal return for years after 1990.

BORROWING FOR COLLEGE

Dear Edith: We are in our sixties, with a retirement income of $55,000 (interest, pension, and social security). We pay an income tax of $4,660.

Our youngest son will be a senior in a private college this fall. Estimated costs for the coming year are $10,000. Would we be wise to take out a loan on our $185,000 debt-free home to pay for his schooling and be able to deduct the interest on our income tax?—Mrs. H.N.

Just because someone wants to lend you money is no reason to take it. And just because you can deduct the interest on your income tax is no reason either.

Sure, you'd have a full income tax deduction. But you'd also have monthly payments to meet. You might have closing costs, and you'd have a long-term debt. Most banks won't bother with $10,000 mortgages anyway, so you'd have to make it a larger loan. As opposed to using some of your own savings, take my word for it, you'd end up behind.

Don't borrow unless you have to.

NEW RULES ON DEPRECIATION

Dear Edith: I used to depreciate my apartment building at 8.8 percent, but the new tax law says depreciation must now be claimed over a period of 27.5 years. What percent of depreciation should I be claiming?—D.B.

The same as you have been using. If you started out depreciating your building on a 15-year basis, you continue with that schedule. The new longer depreciation periods apply to property first put into service after December 31, 1986.

NOT DEDUCTIBLE IN TEXAS

Dear Edith: You wrote that interest on up to $100,000 borrowing against the equity in one's home is deductible on a federal income tax return, no matter what the money is used for. Is this true in Texas? I sure hope so.—Ms. C.V.

Except for home improvements, you cannot borrow against the home you already own in Texas. And unless a loan is secured by the property, the IRS will not let you deduct what it calls consumer interest.

All of which is by way of saying "Sorry, no, it doesn't apply in Texas."

REPAIRS VERSUS IMPROVEMENTS

Dear Edith: My accountant said I should make a distinction between repairs and improvements on the two-family I just bought, but he didn't explain why. Could you give me some information?—H.L.

Your accountant cares about the difference because the Internal Revenue Service cares. Repairs, which keep the property in good condition, may be taken as an immediate expense, before you figure profit on your duplex. Improvements, which add to the value of the property and prolong its life, cannot be taken as an immediate expense. For income tax purposes, the cost of an improvement must be spread over a number of years to come (capitalized).

A complete new roof is an improvement. Patches on the old one are repairs. Painting is a repair, unless it is part of a new room or addition. Replacing defective plumbing is a repair, but replacing iron pipes with copper counts as an improvement. Insulation is a capital improvement; so is installing a new bathroom, paving a driveway and putting in fencing.

Just furnish your accountant with details on each expense, and he will sort it out properly at the end of the year.

DEDUCTING ON VACANT LAND

Dear Edith: I rent a subsidized housing apartment. I found a piece of bare ground, 2-1/2 acres, for sale at a steal. I pay every month. Every time I get my payment card I notice that approximately half of what I am paying is interest. I believe these interest payments are tax-deductible but I'm not sure. I have no other property, a home or anything, so are the payments deductible as an only home?—Mr. H.R.

I'm afraid not. Your home is the apartment you rent. One can also deduct interest paid on a second home, but it must have kitchen and bath facilities to qualify. You can't call vacant land a home.

DEDUCTING A LOT OF INTEREST

Dear Edith: We own a house but plan to build elsewhere when we retire. We have been looking at lots with the thought of buying now but waiting to build. Under the new tax laws, could this lot be a "second home" in order to deduct the interest paid, for income tax purposes? If not, is there some other way to make the interest deductible?—Mr. T.O.

You can deduct your interest under "second home" after construction starts. Before that, it's considered consumer interest.

DEDUCTING SON'S POINTS

Dear Edith: I am thinking of selling my house to my son. Points paid on his mortgage—are they tax-deductible?—Mr. N.Y.

If he buys the place as his own residence, the points he pays are deductible as up-front interest, the year he pays them. If he buys it as investment property, most of his costs of buying, including points, must be deducted bit by bit over a period of years.

If you pay the points, they are not deductible at all because one cannot deduct interest paid on someone else's loan.

CHAPTER 8

Defects and Problems

Every one of these letters describes a different situation, which makes them particularly interesting. Now that they're gathered together, I find the "see a lawyer" advice does seem to recur with some regularity. But that's what I'd do myself—that or small claims court—for most of these problems. On the ones where it's "Darned if I know" I generally don't put them in the paper.

LETTERS I DIDN'T PRINT

Dear Edith: Regarding serious safety hazard which I almost was a victim of a furious snow avalanche from a slate roof adjacent to the house I was visiting . . .notified the owner of the said property, no reply and he does not live here. . . .Building code inspector notified me that the buildings were built prior to the time codes were established and this does not help. . .who would be liable if a vehicle is crushed or a person is killed on your property from a snow avalanche from the adjacent building with the slate roof which is three (3) feet from your line and driveway and the walk to rear door. A wrong exists—it must be corrected—moral law I would say—but how?

Beats me.

Dear Edith: I just bought my house in a lovely neighborhood that I'm proud to be part of. My neighbor who has three dogs does nothing in the way of restraining them and their droppings. . .he states his dogs are not the only ones in my yard, his fence is dug under by the dogs, and finally that he would in no way tie the dogs. . . .to add to it his son is my district councillor on the city council. Help!!!

Not much I could think of to suggest, on that one. But I knew the answer to the next one for sure.

Dear Ms. Lank: Would you please write and tell us how to go about putting a lean on a piece of property? Very truly yours.

If the problem is a lean, I usually suggest propping the building up with 2×4s and calling in an engineer. But some I just can't answer:

Dear Edith Lank: I have property in Dutchess County which according to town codes is not buildable land...about 10 acres.... I was wondering if the land could be used for a veterans' cemetery. Any information you might have will be appreciated. Thank you for your time.

ELECTRIC LINES OVER THE POOL

Dear Edith: We bought a house in November. There is a pool and a hot tub in the backyard. Recently a friend came out and said the lights surrounding the pool and tub were too close. He suggested we get the town's electrical inspector to come out and take a look because if someone got hurt, our insurance wouldn't cover it if the lights weren't up to code.

The inspector came out and said not only were the lights wrong, but the overhead electric, phone and cable lines were not supposed to be over the pool. Now we have a violation because of overhead lines, lighting too close, and lines that should be moved underground to various outlets. This is going to cost us thousands of dollars. Can we sue the former owners because they never got permits? Can we sue the company that installed the hot tub incorrectly? Can we get the violations corrected without paying for it out of our own pocket? It's not right that we should be stuck with this. —Mr. and Mrs. E.A.

The legal question is complex, and one factor may be that you could have seen the violations before you bought. A lawyer can advise whether you have any claim on the seller or the installer. In the meantime, insurance considerations aside, just thank your lucky stars a friend steered you in the right direction before someone got killed.

BUYING LAND OUT OF TOWN

Dear Edith: We have bought acreage in Tennessee by mail (after one trip there). We asked for a survey with the sale and received a ten-year-old one. It did not show three acres that was supposed to be included in the sale. The owner, an older man, honestly thought he owned the extra land, but he didn't. We then sent a large retainer to a local attorney but it got us only a letter in return advising us we had no recourse.

We feel we have been taken so much we want to avoid this again and want a checklist to follow so none of these expensive errors will happen when we buy a different homestead. I am sure many out-of-town buyers are experiencing this sort of thing. —Mrs. F.P.

I hope not.

The whole point of the survey is to find out ahead of time exactly what you are going to purchase. If you had used the attorney right at the beginning, he or she would have insisted on a current survey, and would have alerted you to the missing three acres before you turned over the money.

Next time, call in a lawyer at the start. Attorneys have just the checklists you want.

HOLES IN GARAGE ROOF

Dear Edith: We recently purchased our first home. We were told the garage roof was in good condition but we could not get into the garage because the keys were not available. When we inspected just before closing we could not see the inside of the roof because doors and building materials were stored at the ceiling.

After the sellers moved we were appalled to discover several holes in the roof. The broker and our attorney both claim we bought the place "as is." What are our rights?—R. and S.T.

You may or may not have a case against those who told you the roof was in good shape. The cost of a garage roof is probably not enough to warrant paying for a lawyer's valuable time, though. Why not try small claims court (usually up to $1,500 or $2,000) yourselves? It's a simple, inexpensive procedure, and you'll get a judge's opinion.

MOVING THAT FENCE

Dear Edith: Years ago I bought a vacant lot from a local real estate broker who had just purchased it from the adjacent property owner. A fence separated the two properties, however it encroached on my property by about ten feet. I was assured by the broker that he would get the previous owner to move the fence in a few short weeks or have it done at his own expense if necessary.

After six years the fence is still there and in the meantime the property next door has a different owner. My broker friend during all this time managed to write three letters asking the owner to move the fence. Now he says the matter is out of his hands and I should sue the new neighbor.

Whose responsibility is it to move the fence and what is your opinion about the length of time my broker friend sat on this? What do you think?—Mr. M.L.

I think you should have had a lawyer handle the matter from the beginning, and I think you should talk to one immediately. It's more than a matter of moving the fence; you may be in danger of losing ownership of that strip of land.

FHA AND THE FUSE BOX

Dear Edith: In November I bought my first home. We went FHA and were told FHA would send over an inspector so I need not spend the money to have an engineer do it. I thought the fuse box was questionable, having only five circuits for a large colonial.

So now an electrician told us to replace it immediately as it is very overloaded. We are putting in 13 separate lines to replace those five.

I have spoken to the lender and two lawyers and cannot get an answer. Do I have any recourse to have FHA pay for the repairs since the problem was not caught by its inspector?—Sincerely, "Almost up in smoke"

No recourse. The FHA says it does the best it can, but makes no guarantees about its inspections. Sorry.

FRIDGE IN THE BASEMENT

Dear Edith: When I bought this house, the contract said the sellers would leave it clean, which they didn't. I have this big refrigerator in my basement. I called my lawyer and told him about it; he said do you want me to come over and move it? Edith, can I have my lawyer get this family to remove this big refrigerator out of my basement?—C.V.

I'm afraid the time to settle the matter was before you handed over the money for the house. It's always wise to make a last-minute inspection of the property on your way to the closing, and your right to do so should have been included in the sales contract.

After settlement, it's a case of "you bought it, you got it" for many matters. You might try the simple inexpensive remedy of small claims court, asking that the sellers to pay the cost of disposal.

Until you remove the refrigerator, please do take the door off its hinges. Those things can be death traps for small children.

CLOSING AGENT FAULTY

Dear Edith: Last year I purchased a home with normal closing procedures. Now I found out the property was never transferred to my name. Tax bills were sent to the previous owner who did not send them on to me. I ended up paying penalties and late charges. The person who ran the closing did not help me. I don't think it was fair.—Ms. S.Q.

As you realized, an owner is responsible for property taxes whether the bill reaches the right person or not.

If the property is still not in your name, you're in serious trouble and need a lawyer's help. If the problem has been cleared up, small claims court is ideal for your situation: simple and inexpensive. You can get a judge's opinion on whether the person who ran the closing was negligent and should pay your extra costs.

SUPPORTING BEAMS CRACKED

Dear Edith: The latter part of 1986, my son took a VA as-is mortgage on a two-story house. It was rehabbed by the previous owner. Now an inspector told him that the back porch had to be torn down to put supporting beams in, and the basement needs three beams as the ones there are cracked. Please tell me what, if anything, he should do. Thank you kindly.—H. O'S.

Your son should replace the beams.

When he bought "as is," he agreed to take any problems along with the house.

NO DEED, NO NOTHING

Dear Edith: In December, 1982, my husband and I bought two weeks of time at a resort in Freeport, Grand Bahama. We made a deposit and sent the entire balance upon our return home as per our purchase agreement. We have continued to use these weeks each year but we never got ownership papers from the lawyer handling it for the owners. We received excuses even when we went to see him last December when we were down there.

In March my husband died suddenly and now I very much need to sell something I cannot prove I own. I have written this lawyer and the time-share seller and have not received the courtesy of a reply. What is my next recourse? Should I have my lawyer intervene? Is there any document I can offer as legal proof of ownership should I find a buyer?—H.H.

We can't assume that you do own that time-share.

Merely sending someone money didn't give you title. You're right; any prudent buyer will want you to prove ownership. But were you prudent when you bought? Did you insist on legal proof of ownership from the person who sold to you?

You should have operated through your own lawyer (in the Bahamas) right from the start. That way, you wouldn't have turned over the money until you received proof of clear title, and a deed or whatever other papers were appropriate.

You must certainly work through an attorney at this point. Start by asking advice from the one who is handling your husband's estate, and be prepared to retain a lawyer in the Bahamas.

THOSE LIGHT BULBS

Dear Edith: You said in your column that some home buyers were upset because the sellers removed the light bulbs from the ceiling fixtures. Back when I was in college, our business law teacher (a lawyer) told us that whatever was permanently affixed to the real property automatically became part of the real estate. Are light bulbs considered "permanently affixed" and therefore not removable?—Ms. B.

How would you regard the front door key, and the little remote gadget that operates the garage door opener? They haven't been affixed at all, but were certainly intended to become part of the real estate.

You learned a good general rule for the creation of a fixture (personal property that becomes part of the real estate). "Annexation" is not, however, the only test of a fixture. "Intention" is also considered; was the item meant to become a permanent part of the real estate?

I picked the light bulbs to illustrate the way some buyers and sellers get hung up on trivial items. To settle your question, we'd have to look for past court rulings, and I hope no one's ever been petty enough to start a lawsuit over light bulbs. These disputes can become so emotional, though, that nothing would surprise me.

ASSESSED VALUE DIFFERS

Dear Edith: I bought my house over a year ago. I told the real estate agent I wouldn't pay more than the appraised value for the house. Now my property tax bill shows the house appraised for $12,000 less than I paid. Please explain the difference. I am afraid I will have to take a big loss when I try to sell my house. What can I do?—Mr. C.S.

You can stop worrying. No matter how conscientious a tax assessor is, the figure arrived at is almost never the same as real market value.

If you placed a mortgage to buy the property, you had the protection of a bank appraisal. Your lender must have determined that the place furnished enough security for the loan you sought.

CHAPTER 9

Decisions, Decisions

"Should we put our son's name on the deed?"

Most of these decisions are about whether to refinance a mortgage, and—one of my pet topics—whether to put one's house in the children's names.

SELLING AND RENTING

Dear Edith: I've lived in my present home for 35 years. It's been paid for a long time. I'm retired, my husband works part-time and also receives Social Security. Second marriage for us both.

I'm thinking about selling my house. What do you think about me putting the entire amount in the bank and paying rent for an apartment with the interest from the money?—L.S.

I think it's a fine idea, if apartment living is what you want. Too many older folks who would really like to move feel tied to a big house because "it's free and clear and costs me almost nothing." Staying put is great if that's what they want, but they don't realize they are free to do as you suggest. Because they paid relatively little for the house many years ago, they can't realize how much they'd have if they sold.

You won't put the money into a low-interest day-to-day account, of course, but rather into the highest possible CDs or long-term Treasury bills.

BETTER IN THE LONG RUN

Dear Edith: For older people, is it really better to sell their house and pay rent on an apartment with the interest from the proceeds? If they live to a good age, say in the 80s or 90s, wouldn't they be losing in the long run? —Mrs. O.A.E.

At that age, one should be living in the most comfortable manner one can afford. For some people, that means staying in the old homestead, or buying something smaller with one's own backyard and lawn.

For others, apartment living means being free of many cares. The older person who is in a position to choose should base the decision on comfort rather than financial considerations.

WOULDN'T HAVE TO MOVE

Dear Edith: I would like to get in touch with Mrs. S.N. who said she can't afford to stay in her house. I'd like to buy it. I am a widow and I am looking for a place to live. She does not have to move. She can live with me. I would like to know how much she wants for her house. I would like a picture of it. How many rooms and what kind of heat? I have a certain amount of cash. Thank you. —Mrs. K.H.

Sorry, but I can't forward your offer.

Sharing housing with other older people can be a fine solution to many problems. Bring the matter up at a senior citizens' service center. I hope you turn up something.

EARLY LOAN PAYOFF

Dear Edith: We purchased our home in June 1964 with a 30-year FHA mortgage. The amount of the loan was $11,500. The interest rate was five percent.

Last week we received a statement showing a balance on the principal of $3,799. Would we be smart to pay off the loan now? If so, how much would we be saving in interest? —Mr. and Mrs. R.H.

If you pay off your loan now, you won't be saving any interest. You'll be losing the interest your $3,799 could be earning elsewhere. If you could find a long-term CD earning 9 percent, you'd be ahead, at the end of the year, by a whole $152 (before income tax).

There is, of course, something called psychic income, the emotional satisfaction of having your home free and clear. If that's worth $152 a year to you, forget what I just said and go for it.

PAYING OFF THAT MORTGAGE

Dear Edith: Our accountant has recommended that we should pay off our 9.5 percent mortgage, which still has 23 years to go. We are not so sure.

It is something we would be able to do by withdrawing money from a savings account. I am 70 years old, my wife is 57 and still working. We have always been under the impression that we needed the interest deduction for our income taxes. Please give us your opinion. —Mr. and Mrs. L.O'B.

Your accountant knows your whole financial position, so I won't tell you which way to go. I can set you straight on one thing.

The money you'd take out of savings to pay off the mortgage is presently earning taxable income somewhere. After you use it to pay off the mortgage, you will lose the tax deduction of paying mortgage interest, but you'll also have less taxable interest to declare as income. So don't worry about the income tax aspect of your decision—it's pretty much a wash, either way you go.

PAID OFF AT A DISCOUNT

Dear Edith: I was surprised at your response to a widow who asked whether she should pay off her 5.25 percent mortgage. You should have emphasized that she has three choices, not two.

The first is to continue the present payment schedule. The second is to pay off the principal in one payment, as she wanted. Most banks will accept that payment.

The third choice is to offer to pay off the principal with a discount to help the bank get a low-interest loan off its books.

I recently went through this exercise myself and it worked. —Mr. H.B.B.

I was preparing to reply that few lending institutions will discuss a discount these days. Often the mortgage has long since been sold to a secondary lender out of town.

But it appears you pulled it off, so what the heck—I'm publishing your story for the benefit of those who might want to try.

COULDN'T GET A DISCOUNT

Dear Edith: In May, 1985 I wrote my mortgage company asking if they would honor a modest discount if we paid off our home loan. Their reply was that an investor held the mortgage and was not interested in converting our 7.5% loan to some other investment at a higher rate. What would you have done done in this matter?—Mr. P.A.

I'd have accepted the turndown. If they don't want to give you a discount, they don't have to. Then I'd have taken that payoff money and put it into something paying more than 7.5 percent (which was an option when interest rates were higher in 1985). I hope you did just that.

Mortgage banking is a complicated matter, with large packages of loans sold over and over again on the secondary market. What might sound like

DOCUMENTS AT PAYOFF

Dear Edith: I will be making the final payment on my home mortgage and would like to know what the bank should provide as documentation, what and who should have the documents recorded. —K.D.C.

The bank should send you a certificate of satisfaction, which you should file to clear the record of the loan.

If the bank has been keeping money in escrow for your property taxes and insurance, it owes you an accounting and return of your money. And if it has your abstract (that thick wad of papers with the legal history of your land) you want that also.

If you have an FHA mortgage, the bank should notify HUD of the payoff, because you may be due for a partial refund of mortgage insurance premiums.

Most lenders have systems set up to cover all these matters, but it won't hurt to phone and ask.

RECORDING MORTGAGE SATISFACTION

Dear Edith: Recently I paid off my mortgage. I would like to know what you mean by "be sure to have it entered in the public records" as in the clipping I have enclosed. Would you please explain how or what must be done?—Mr. W.O'B.

The document I referred to is a certificate of satisfaction, your lender's acknowledgment that the debt is paid off. In some states, it takes the form of a release deed.

You are entitled to receive this paper. Private lenders don't always realize they owe it to you, and you may need to press for it, or even have a lawyer intervene.

A lending institution, on the other hand, will probably send you the certificate as a matter of routine. Problem is, it may be buried among other papers you receive at the same time—abstract of title, original mortgage document, final accounting or escrow account records. Many people put the works in a drawer or wastebasket and forget the whole thing.

That's where the trouble starts, because it is important that the public records show the debt has been cleared. Unless the bank has recorded the certificate for you, do it yourself. You simply take it to the public recorder (in most areas, your county clerk), and pay a small fee.

WHO PAYS FOR CERTIFICATE?

Dear Edith: When I paid off a second mortgage, the lawyer who handled things said I was to pay for drawing up the certificate of satisfaction. Since I needed it I paid, but I have often wondered why they told me it was my expense. Who should pay for the certificate? – Dr. R.D.

It's customary for the mortgagee (lender) to pay for preparing the document. The mortgagor (borrower) then pays to have it recorded. The borrower might be asked to stand the whole expense when the loan is being paid off early, or when the lender is a private party.

PAYING OFF THE LOAN

Dear Edith: In a couple of months I will make the last payment on my mortgage. Hurray!
What takes place at that time? I vaguely recall that some sort of document needs to be filed with the county clerk. Additionally, how do I go about getting the escrow account returned to me so I can be in control of the funds set aside to pay taxes? Will it be necessary to engage a lawyer? – Mr. F.B., Jr.

A regular lending institution will have systems set up to take care of giving you that certificate of satisfaction (the document that should be entered in the public records) and returning the balance in your escrow account. A lawyer is more likely to be necessary when you are dealing with a private party.

$25 FOR A CERTIFICATE

Dear Edith: My mortgage will be paid up on September 1. The bank told me that I will get a certificate of satisfaction and it will cost me $25. Why must I pay this? Should not the bank give it to me without cost?
Also I am the holder of a mortgage on property I sold, also to be paid up on September 1. I will have to give the borrower a satisfaction certificate. How do I go about getting it? Will I be obliged to pay $25? – Mr. K.B.R.

I wouldn't be suprised if you ended up getting stuck on both ends.

The mortgage document you originally gave the bank probably contains some agreement about who will pay for preparing that certificate. If the lender will send it along only after receiving $25, spend the money. It's important.

As for the other mortgage: Again, I don't know what you obligated yourself to when you signed the loan papers. Your borrower is probably entitled to the certificate when the last payment is made, and you'll want a lawyer to draw it up.

REFINANCING VA LOAN

Dear Edith: I have a home I purchased three years ago using a VA loan. My interest rate is 12.5 percent. Should I refinace the loan? What steps do I take? —Mr. K.V.

If you plan to remain in the house for two years or more and can drop your interest rate by at least 2 percent, it usually pays to refinance. You will have to pay substantial closing costs and points. Go in and discuss the whole thing with your mortgage lender.

If it's an out-of-town institution, find a local lender handling VA mortgages and talk the matter over here. An interviewer should be able to give you figures on what a refinance would cost, whether you could include some of those charges in a larger loan, and how many months it would take to recoup your outlay.

NEW RULE ON VA REFINANCE

Dear Edith: I was told I can't refinance with the VA because of a new law. How is this an advantage for us vets?—Mr. C.P.

You can still refinance your present home with a VA mortgage. The recent change limits your borrowing to 90 percent of present market value, instead of the previous 100 percent.

GOING PRICE IN NEIGHBORHOOD

Dear Edith: We bought an older home in need of repairs. Some were major like windows, but how do you know when you're putting too much money in the house? We have made a few repairs with our likes in mind but we don't want to exceed the going prices in the neighborhood. Maybe you could give us some guidelines.—E.W.

You've answered your own question; you already know the basic guideline. It's financially unwise to improve a house so that it's more elaborate or expensive than its neighbors. A given street will usually support only a given price. After that, buyers with more to spend typically want to live in a more prestigious area.

Illogical, but a fact of human nature. Real estate appraisers even have a Latin term for buyers' preference as to area—*situs*.

With questions on specific improvements, call a real estate broker who is active in your neighborhood, for a little free advice.

KEEP IT OR SELL?

Dear Edith: Our house is mortgage free. But for a job reason we will have to move to another city. Should we rent the house and buy another with mortgage payments? Should we sell it and use the money as a down payment for another house?—R.P.

Don't keep the house and rent it out. Being a landlord is a challenging job, even if you live nearby. You don't want to try it for the first time from a distance.

IMPROVING THEIR CAPE COD

Dear Edith: We live in a two-bedroom Cape Cod that is 20 years old and we purchased for $60,000 in 1986. We are contemplating making improvements to provide us with more needed space for the future versus purchasing a larger home. The house has 1,000 square feet with an attached garage that could be made into a family room and we also have a spacious unfinished attic that could be converted. How much do improvements of this nature add to the value of your home? Are we better off looking to invest our money in purchasing a larger home?—D.T.

The answer depends on your neighborhood. Is yours the most modest house on the street? If your neighbors also have Cape Cods, what have they done about enlarging their homes? It is not financially prudent to make yours the most expensive house in the area.

Then, how fond are you of the neighborhood? And what about your financial situation? Ages? Earning potential? Long-range plans? How long do you see yourselves staying in a larger home?

You can see there's no one right answer. The most important factor is probably the average size and market value of other houses on the street, as compared with your home.

If you aren't certain about price levels and sizes in your area, a nearby real estate office can give you some data on recent sales.

$600,000 TAX-FREE

Dear Edith: Before I sign over my house to my daughter, I'd like to know how much I can leave in my will before an estate tax would be due.—Mr. D.W.

Up to $600,000 may be transferred by gift during your lifetime or at death, without any federal gift or estate tax. The amount is in addition to any gifts or bequests to a spouse, which are free of federal taxes.

State regulations vary, but the federal rules at least are generous and simple.

TAKING OVER THE HOUSE

Dear Edith: My mother tells me according to her will I will inherit her house. Right now her name and my father's name is on the deed. He passed away three years ago.

We would like to know what to do about getting my name on the deed now, instead of waiting until I inherit the house. By not having it done now, might it not take longer and more legal stuff to do it then?

Can we just go to the recorder's office and have the change made?—Mrs. N.H.

Your mother transfers the house by having a lawyer draw up a deed for her to sign. The attorney can then help you put it in the county records.

Consider, though. If you get the house as a gift now, your cost basis is the same as your folks'. If you sold, you'd probably have a large taxable capital gain.

And if your mother decided to move out and sell, she couldn't take the special home-owners' tax treatment on the profit, because it wouldn't be her house any more.

If you wait to inherit the house, you get it with a new cost basis, current value. If you sold soon after, you'd have little or no taxable profit.

GIVING THE HOUSE TO SON

Dear Edith: This is a beautiful Saturday afternoon and the wife and I are sitting in the backyard reading and discussing life in general. I was reading your column and it brought up our home and taxes.

If something happened to one of us the other would automatically get the house, we know that. No tax involved.

But how does the remaining spouse go about giving the house to our son? We know how to do it with our other assets, stocks etc. This of course would be to avoid probate and any taxes involved.—Mr. V.S.T.

One is allowed to give during a lifetime or leave at death up to $600,000 with no federal tax due ever (and that's besides anything given or left to a spouse, which transfers tax-free). If you give ownership to your son, you won't owe a gift tax but you'll have that much less you can leave tax-free at death; it's a combined gift and inheritance tax exclusion.

From your son's point of view: If he receives the house as a gift, he takes over your cost basis, which is probably low. If he waits to inherit it, he gets a stepped-up basis, value at the time of death.

Then again, what if your son went bankrupt, became divorced, or died? Your home might be caught up in complications. And if in the future you wanted to sell, you would have lost the chance to take up to $125,000 profit tax-free, if the place were no longer your property.

Probate costs and inheritance taxes aren't anywhere near as terrible as most people fear, and you can tell that I don't like the idea of turning one's home over during a lifetime.

But on the other side: You can give any individual up to $10,000 a year without any gift tax; you and your wife could transfer up to $40,000 a year to your son and his wife without using up any of that $600,000 entitlement. If you think your combined estates will go beyond the $600,000 figure, talk with an attorney who specializes in estate planning about whether any gifts are appropriate now. You'd want a lawyer in any event, to prepare the deed necessary to transfer ownership of the house.

WHY THE LAWYER DID IT

Dear Edith: I read a letter recently in your column concerning inherited property versus property signed over to sons or daughters before a parent dies.

My wife's mother signed over a lake home purchased in the 1950s for about $10,000. You seem to indicate that if we sell the property for $100,000 after her death, we will have to pay income tax on $90,000 less improvements. But if we inherited it through her will, the tax would be much less or none at all.

If that's so, why would a lawyer have advised her to sign over the property now?—Mr. K.C.

I don't know. I'm not a lawyer, I wasn't there, and I don't know what other considerations might have prompted the advice—a very large estate, possibility of a contested will, health costs, or some other factors.

My original income tax information is correct, though.

FEDERAL ESTATE TAX EXCLUSION

Dear Edith: In an item "Mother Has No Will" you state that with a will there is no federal inheritance tax up to $600,000. I thought that amount applied to only married couples, not to offspring. Please clarify.—Mrs. K.R.

Although it isn't really a matter of real estate, I'll be happy to clear up a couple of your misconceptions.

First, estate tax regulations are the same whether or not there is a will.

Then, the rules have changed over the past decade or so. There is now no federal gift or estate tax on anything given to a spouse, during life or at death. No dollar limit.

In addition, a total of $600,000 may be given to other persons, as gifts during a lifetime and/or inheritance at death, with no federal tax due.

CHAPTER 10

That FHA Refund

"The refund was $1,491.58. Holy smoke!"

Perhaps it's the guys on cable TV, getting everyone excited about money the government may owe people. In that past couple of years there's been an explosion of letters about the possibility of refunded insurance premiums for paid-up FHA mortgages.

The money is technically known as a distributive share of unused premiums, and is different from the refund of a specific percentage of the lump-sum MIP (mortgage insurance premium) now being charged when newer FHA loans are made.

These letters discuss the general rules, recount successful experiences, then take up the question of becoming a finder or tracer of lost funds. They end up with a group of hopeful—and disappointed—VA borrowers.

GOVERNMENT OWES MONEY

Dear Edith: Is it correct that if an FHA mortgage is paid off I'm reimbursed by a federal agency if notified by me or mortgage company? I also understand that there are millions of dollars the government is holding for citizens in various claims such as bank accounts, stocks, insurance premiums etc. Can I consider this to be true?—B.G.

Yes, it's true. The government does hold funds for people who can't be located. Much of it is in those insurance premium distributive shares, which are due on some—not all—paid-off FHA mortgages.

The person paying off an FHA mortgage, whether at the end of the term or before that, may be due a rebate for unused mortgage insurance premiums. It all depends on how long the mortgage has been in force, and how healthy the pool of insurance premiums is for mortgages placed that year—whether there have been many foreclosures in that particular group.

The borrower should hear from the FHA within a few months after the loan is closed out. Lenders are supposed to notify the FHA, but they sometimes don't bother. Or the borrower may have sold and moved with no forwarding address.

There used to be a six-year statute of limitations; if you hadn't followed up in time, you lost your claim to a refund. A few years ago, though, that cut-off date was eliminated. If you think you might be due a refund on an old FHA mortgage you paid off, write to HUD. You may be due nothing, but it's worth investigating.

To research it yourself, write to HUD, Distributive Shares Branch, Room 2239, 451 Seventh Street S.W., Washington, D.C., 20401. The phone number is 202/755-5616.

LIFE AND DISABILITY INSURANCE

Dear Edith: How would I go about collecting a refund on the mortgage insurance I paid for 21 years? I paid $6.83 a month for all those years. It was listed as "Life and/or Disability Insurance." Would this be the same as FHA mortgage insurance?—E.V.

No, it wouldn't. No refund due. Sorry.

FHA MORTGAGE REFUND

Dear Edith: Recently I attended one of those free real estate investment seminars. The speaker mentioned that a person may be entitled to reimbursement of the mortgage insurance. Is this true? How do you go about doing it? I've had an FHA mortgage for 4 years and am not selling the house.—Mr. F.W.

No distributive share or refund is due while the loan is still in force.

DOESN'T SEEM FAIR

Dear Edith: We bought a house in 1974 with an FHA mortgage. Last year we sold the house and the buyer assumed our mortgage. When the new owner pays off the mortgage, will we be entitled to a share of the insurance premium refund?—Ms. M.D.

In those cases where a distribution is due, it goes to the person making the last payment. It wouldn't matter if someone else had been making payments for 29 years; the current owner of the property, who makes the last payment, receives the money.

Doesn't seem fair, does it?

REFUND OF MIP

Dear Edith: I recently bought a house and at time of closing was charged $3,321 for mortgage insurance premium (MIP), covering the life of the 30-year mortgage. If I do sell this house three or five years from now and pay off the mortgage, do I get part of that money back?—Mr. G.H.

It sounds as if you have an FHA loan, one of the newer ones that require that lump-sum mortgage insurance premium. If you paid off the mortgage after three years, you would get back approximately 70 percent; after five years, about half.

The FHA, or rather its parent agency, HUD, makes a distinction between this *refund* and the *distributive share* sometimes due on the payoff of longer-lasting mortgages.

HAD AN FHA LOAN

Dear Edith: A friend told me if someone sells a home which had an FHA mortgage they may have a refund coming. I sold a house which had an FHA mortgage in 1986 which I owned for 17 years. Would this apply to me?—Mr. B.L.

It isn't selling the house that counts, but making the last payment on the loan. If you paid yours off when you sold, you may have a distributive share (not technically a refund) coming. If the loan was assumed by your buyer, the money could be due in the future, but would go to that buyer.

ELUSIVE FHA INSURANCE REFUND

Dear Edith: Have you ever known anyone who actually received this elusive FHA insurance refund? We had an FHA mortgage from March 1983 to December 1987, when we paid it off. I phoned HUD, someone in the office said we would be entitled to a refund. Our lender was under the impression we were entitled. When we applied, HUD said "No refund." I eventually wrote the assistant secretary of HUD, who replied that our mortgage had not lasted long enough for a refund.

I wonder if anyone has ever received this reimbursement.—Ms. S.D.

Yes, I have heard from readers who did receive the refund. To most it came as a complete surprise, because the paperwork is usually handled as a matter of course by lenders.

One phone call to HUD would have brought you the information that an FHA loan must be a certain age (at the moment, about seven years old or older) when it is paid off, to qualify for a distributive share. At times during the past it had to be at least 12 years old.

VERY NICE SURPRISE

Dear Edith: I received a check on an FHA refund in the amount of $1,019 from a 30-year mortgage terminated in June, 1988. It came automatically and was a very nice surprise. (The original amount of the loan was $11,000 at 5.25 percent.) —S.M.T.

DON'T MISS FHA REFUND

Dear Edith: You have written on the FHA refund possibility several times and we thank you. My loan was initiated in 1955. We paid it off when there was enough in the escrow account to pay off the remaining balance. The FHA refund was $1,491.58. Holy smoke! Don't let people miss this. —D.D.

GOT MORE THAN HE PAID

Dear Edith: Thanks to information in your column, I recently received an FHA refund in the amount of $991.54 in connection with a 25-year mortgage that matured in August 1988. (Originally borrowed $13,050 at 5.25 percent.)

This may not have enough general interest to include in your column, but readers might be interested to learn that the refund can be substantial.

I unearthed a copy of the amortization schedule and was surprised to learn that the total mortgage insurance premiums paid during the life of the loan amounted to $988.68. I received more of a refund than I paid.

I am reluctant to look this particular gift horse too carefully in the mouth by writing FHA to question the apparent display of fiscal irresponsibility. I cannot fathom how the agency could be at risk for 25 years and not use up any part of the original premium. —Mr. S.K.O.

The FHA doesn't just sit on the money collected as premiums. The sums are invested, and 25 years is a long time. Even in a simple bank account, one dollar you sent the FHA back in 1963 would more than double twice over in that time. Losses could be paid out of the insurance pool, with substantial sums still left. The Federal Housing Administration is one of the few government agencies that pays for itself and comes out in the black almost every year.

Yes, your letter is of general interest, because readers keep writing in to ask if anyone actually collects that refund.

$1,200 REFUND FROM FHA

Dear Edith: You had an article in the paper last winter about the government owing some people refunded mortgage insurance premiums on paid-off FHA mortgages. You mentioned people that ask for "finders' fees." We had someone contact us by mail in January, saying the government owed us money and wanting 10 percent of anything they collected for us. Then a telephone call in February from someone asking 50 percent.

Because of your article I dug up our old FHA case number and wrote to the address in your article. They replied that we were not entitled to a refund. But I decided to pursue the matter.

I called a local FHA (HUD) office and guess what! Our name was on the next HUD list coming out. We have $1,200 coming.

Why didn't the government ever contact us? We are still at the same address after 32 years. And how did anyone get our name before it came out on the FHA lists? We could easily have been convinced there was no way to find the money without help. —Mrs. K.T.

Most people do hear from the FHA routinely. Some get lost in the cracks as you did.

If one pays off a long-standing FHA loan and hasn't heard anything within four months, it's worth contacting the lending institution or writing to HUD directly. Those lists come out two years after the loans are paid off, by the way.

RAN INTO A STONE WALL

Dear Edith: I ran into a stone wall. I assumed an FHA mortgage and eventually paid it off. I sent HUD all the numbers that appear on the mortgage, the bank's loan number, liber and page number from the register of deeds department, title insurance policy number and still they say I can't obtain a refund on unused FHA insurance premiums without the FHA case number. Have you any idea where I could find that magic number? I am retired, no pension, only social security and could use the money. —F.H.

You found the catch—one has to have the FHA case number. The HUD hot line suggests looking in the public records at the county clerk's office; sometimes the mortgage document does mention the FHA number.

If there was a real estate office involved when you bought, perhaps their papers would have your FHA case number. Or if you could locate the very first borrowers, perhaps they saved their paperwork. Otherwise, it's true—no FHA case number, no possibility of refund.

WHERE TO FIND FHA CASE NUMBER

Dear Edith: People who are looking for the FHA case number on their mortgages ought to see whether they have the original appraisal report on the property. It contains the case number. Also, the FHA issues case numbers in sequence and the search can be narrowed somewhat if the FHA regional office records are available to identify numbers issued around the time the original mortgages were placed.—H.H.

HUD in Washington can tell people what two digits their particular case number should start with—so they'll know it when they find it. That's useful because the FHA number is not always identified as such.

IT'S FOR REAL

Dear Edith: A television program on cable was a talk show on how to make money by locating people who have money coming to them from the FHA. Is this for real?—Ms. B.D.

Yes, it's for real. The Freedom of Information Act has opened records to "tracers" who ask finder's fees, and the FHA has ruled that those entitled can claim the money no matter how far back.

Many states set limits on the percentage that can be charged as a fee by finders or tracers; some states require registration of finders.

BECOMING REFUND TRACERS

Dear Edith: You asked what experience people had had who wanted to become tracers for money the government owes people.

We purchased the book on how to become a tracer of unclaimed FHA mortgage insurance and also paid the government $125 for a list of names of individuals due refunds.

We prepared and mailed 50 letters to people whose current address matched the address listed on the government list. We followed up with telephone calls in seven days and were able to contact about 30 of those we had mailed letters to.

Several had already received refunds one, two or three years prior. The remainder were unwilling to pay the fee for our services.

Personally we think the sale of this material is a rip-off. Incidentally, the author of the book we purchased is now touting his latest venture "How To Obtain Government Loans."—J.L.

YET ANOTHER TRACER

Dear Edith: I bought a $40 tracer book advertised on TV. The method suggested in the book is very involved, and after locating the missing recipient, the difficulty begins.

It seems HUD refunds the mortgage insurance premiums directly to the FHA borrower. Then comes the catch, getting paid by the borrower for your help. I worked five years in a medical clinic and experienced the difficulty of collecting doctor fees that were paid by insurance directly to the patient. Once people have the money in hand, it is extremely difficult to get them to send your share.

Please, if you have any positive responses, send the word.—L.

Everything so far is negative, but to be fair—those who may have had good experiences may just not be sharing with us. Perhaps they'd rather keep it to themselves?

IT'S A TOTAL RIP-OFF

Dear Edith: You asked for feedback from someone who had become a tracer of FHA refund money. I sent for the book and tape "How To Make $1,000 Cash Every Day" in October and followed that with a payment to HUD for a listing of potential recipients. I made up computerized letters as instructed in the book and tape, and sent them out. I never heard from any of them and one was returned "Address Unknown."

I had one personal encounter from the list, a co-worker who agreed verbally to pay the fee for my service but would never sign the papers to get started with the process. I believe she and her husband probably obtained the refund on their own after I alerted her that she was entitled.

In theory the tracer business sounds wonderful. But I believe it's a total rip-off and a moderately expensive lesson. Also the TV program listed two telephone numbers to call for assistance at any time. After trying those numbers for several days I gave up. I spent a total of $119.85 plus many hours of my time and phone calls to HUD in Washington.—D.B.

LETTERS FROM TRACERS

Dear Edith: We have received three letters lately from people claiming to be finders, locaters and tracers, who have knowlege of money owed my husband's deceased mother and father from an FHA loan made back in the 60s. It is around $400 and these people all wish to charge finders' fees of from 10 percent to 40 percent. I am wondering if there is an agency to whom my husband can write direct and claim the money?—Mrs. D.T.

Call the FHA at the HUD phone number in Washington, 202/755-5616.

ALL THOSE WASTED STAMPS

Dear Edith: After receiving numerous phone calls and 40 letters we feel we should write about tracers. We still are getting letters, many with stamped return envelopes. We wondered how our name was obtained and questioned one caller. He said he bought the list from the government.

What a waste of expense and time for these people, since we got our money by writing to the government before we received any of those letters or calls. Some tracers asked for 10 percent, some 20 percent, some even 35 percent of what was due us.

There should be a stop put to this, firstly for selling citizens' names and secondly the lists are outdated and thirdly doesn't the government owe us some interest on the $1,200 of our money they held for over a year and which we had to write and ask for?

Advise your readers not to waste their time and money in becoming a tracer, especially for FHA mortgage insurance refunds.—W. and H.J.

Thanks for the letter. How about we give the government the benefit of the doubt; for all we know your $1,200 did include interest for that extra year.

NO VA REFUND

Dear Edith: Regarding the matter of FHA refunded insurance premiums: I would like to know if a VA loan that was insured also has the refunded premium provision.—Mr. M.L.

PAID OFF VA LOAN

Dear Edith: My son passed away recently and he carried life insurance that paid off his VA loan. I read somewhere that if you paid off your loan early you would get some kind of a rebate. Is there such a thing? His widow certainly could use it.—Mrs. N.H.

VETERAN WANTS REFUND

Dear Edith: I have been reading in your column letters relative to refund on your mortgage insurance premium. I am a senior citizen and only last year paid off a 30-year G.I. mortgage on my home. To whom should I write? Would it be the bank or the Veterans Administration?—K.K.I.

VA mortgages are not insured; they are guaranteed by the government. The borrower does not pay any insurance premiums, and no refund is due when the loan is paid off.

NO VA INSURANCE

Dear Edith: We obtained a VA mortgage in 1964 (just a couple of months to go now). At the time we got letters from them telling us that we must get adequate mortgage insurance coverage on the house. Naturally we did. We received similar letters from them over the years.

It came as a surprise to me to read in your recent column that "the borrower under a VA mortgage pays no mortgage insurance premium." I realize we are responsible for our own ignorance but what about the bank? Are we just out the money? Is it a case of "too bad, you should have known"?—Mrs. N.N.

Let's talk about three kinds of insurance: (1) home-owners (hazard) insurance, (2) mortgage life insurance, and (3) mortgage insurance.

The first, hazard insurance, protects you if, for example, the house burns down. The bank insists you buy it, so that if there's a fire, the loan can be paid off. I'm sure you carried that type of insurance.

The second, mortgage life insurance, makes your monthly payments if you are disabled, or pays off the whole loan if you die. Carrying this protection is optional; you may or may not have it.

The third type, mortgage insurance, protects the lender against loss if you ever fall behind and the place doesn't bring enough at a foreclosure sale to cover the debt. That's the kind FHA borrowers must pay for. Other borrowers who have low down payments often buy it in the form of PMI, private mortgage insurance. VA borrowers don't carry it; I'm sure you haven't been paying for that type.

No refunds on VA mortgages. The items you've seen refer to FHA loans only. Sorry.

SOLD WITH FHA LOAN

Dear Edith: In 1971 we purchased a HUD home and had an FHA mortgage from 1971 until 1984. When we sold our home the buyers assumed our mortgage loan. Does this make them eligible for the insurance refund when they pay off the mortgage? Or should we have gotten it at the time they assumed it? Or when they pay it off do we get part of it?—G.N.

Yes, no and no.

If any refund is due, it goes to the person making the last payment.

CHAPTER 11

Understanding Real Estate Law

"I learned too late what 'et al.' meant...."

Real estate law questions are sometimes the most interesting—each one different, and every one tells a story.

Of course I'm not a lawyer, and feel that I walk a tightrope when it comes to giving legal information. For years I worried about it, and one day when the phone rang and I heard "I'm calling for the Monroe County Bar Association" I was sure I was going to be hauled up for the Unauthorized Practice of Law. But no—I was being honored with a Law Day award! Still haven't got over the scare.

Among the letters I don't print, one in three gets a pretty much standard reply that says (in more polite terms),

"Good grief, I wouldn't touch that with a ten-foot pole. If you'd used a lawyer in the first place, you wouldn't be in this fix. Run, do not walk, to the nearest attorney." And because many people are uncomfortable about lawyers, I add advice on how to locate one, and that "it's perfectly acceptable to ask in advance how much it will cost."

WHAT "ET AL." MEANS

Dear Edith: Ten years ago while stationed in the service in California, I purchased some land back in my hometown. This was my first try at buying land so I didn't know what I was supposed to do. I didn't get a title search and I don't think the seller did either, who by the way is a real estate salesperson. I paid cash so I didn't need a search for a loan company.

Anyway, I was going through the records at the court house and lo and behold, I found out that the land is also owned by a thousand other relatives. I learned too late what "et al." meant behind the previous owner's name. Is

there any hope of getting anything done about this or do I chalk it up to a bad experience?—Mr. M.L.

I hope things aren't as bad as you fear. To find out, have a lawyer in your hometown investigate promptly.

LATE HUSBAND'S NAME

Dear Edith: After 23 years of marriage, our house is still listed in my wife's name and her late husband's. She says it doesn't matter since he's dead. Will I have any legal problem if something happens to her?—Mr. N.S.

Can't tell because I don't know what her husband's will said, and I don't know what her will says. Do you?

PROPERTY IS ABANDONED

Dear Edith: I am holding a second mortgage on residential property that is in default and it is my understanding that this property has been abandoned. I have contacted an out-of-state company that holds the first mortgage by phone three times and left my phone number for their foreclosure department to contact me. They have not answered.

I would like to know what my legal rights and duties are to protect myself.—D.D.

Contact a lawyer immediately, in the area where the property is located. You could foreclose yourself, if you think the place will sell for enough to cover the first loan and the legal costs of foreclosure.

Unpaid real estate taxes could mean a real danger to you; if the place is seized and sold for taxes, that wipes out your claim on it. Looking into that threat will probably be one of your lawyer's first moves.

LOSING THAT PENSION

Dear Edith: I'm 67 years old, my lady friend 65. We can't get married, otherwise my friend would lose a pension from Germany. We would like to buy a condo or small house together. How to go about it? Could it be done like a savings account with two names and survivorship on it?—Mr. V.K.

Yes, two unrelated persons can certainly buy real estate together, and if they choose, in most states they can do it as joint tenants with right of survivorship. The deed must specifically state they are taking ownership that way; it means that when one dies, the other automatically becomes complete owner.

HOUSE IN AUNT'S NAME

Dear Edith: In her will my aunt left me her home. The will has been probated. I have no deed to the home. In the county clerk's office it is still in her name. My lawyer has told me I do not have to have a deed. The taxes and all other information is in my name. — Mr. F.E.

One way to receive ownership is by deed, another is through a will. As for proving ownership in the future, you don't do that with a deed anyhow, but by searching the public records. That will is on file, and anyone searching will see that you are now the owner. If the tax authorities have you listed as owner of record, and your lawyer says that's enough, relax.

HAS ONLY LIFE USE

Dear Edith: My husband has left me the house he owns and which we have been occupying for many years, but only for my lifetime. After that, by the provisions of his will, the house would go to his sister's grandson. But consider: I am already 77 years old and have heart trouble. But I'll be obliged to maintain the house, pay taxes, insurance, live in it (and it's a large place). Is there any advice you can think of to forestall the problems I may face because of my husband's will? — Mrs. N.R.

If you have a life estate, you are a complete owner during your lifetime. But just because you own a house doesn't mean you must live in it. You could rent the place out if you no longer wanted to stay there.

Selling your life interest is another possibility. The logical buyer would be that sister's grandson. Perhaps in the future you'd come to some agreement, accepting a cash payment in return for handing over the place while you were still living — elsewhere.

Or the two of you could join together to sell it and share the proceeds.

WROTE IN LAWYERLY WORDS

Dear Edith: My sister held a mortgage on a house she sold me. After paying for a number of years, I asked her if she would consider a payoff, with a discount, naturally. She agreed most hastily.

So I obtained a document called discharge of mortgage. On the document's face I wrote some lawyerly words such as liber such and such, and page number. Oh yes, I added "heirs" and "no assignment" and all other stuff lawyers fill their pages with.

Last Friday, armed with this paper, I went to her place. On my cashier's check (photocopied) I wrote "mortgage fully discharged, paid in full." And I wrote the same words on the discharge document and on her amortization sheet. She signed them all and so did I.

Since we were both in total agreement, why should I have that discharge paper notarized, and why should I have to pay for the writing of a few words in some "liber"?

Surely there can be no doubt that the mortgage is paid in full. Why should I worry? What better evidence of the payoff could I possible need with all those signatures? Why in the Sam Hill would it necessitate the ministrations of a notary, or the bother and expense of a "recording"?—Mr. C.R.

As far as you and your sister are concerned (lawyers would say "as between you and your sister"), that mortgage is certainly paid off. The problem arises when someone else gets involved.

What if your sister's kids, after her death, in all innocence asked payment from your kids? What if you weren't around then?

Or suppose I wanted to buy the property from you. I'd search the public records and refuse to take the place with a loan out against it. Besides, my bank won't give me a loan because the records show the place already has a mortgage.

Then you'd show me your papers.

Now, your sister knows that's her signature, and you know it. But how does my bank know? How do I know? I'd only believe it if a notary authorized by the state saw your sister's identification, watched her sign, heard her swear it was her signature. And if your sister dies—or moves to Australia—you could end up with a legal problem that'd cost more than the cost of recording.

Putting the discharge on record protects you. But the county will accept for recording only those documents that are acknowleged (notarized). They must also be in proper form, so I hope your lawyerly words make enough sense to pass muster.

LAWYER SAYS NO WILL

Dear Edith: I am 58 years young and have two children, a boy 34 and and a girl 38. I own my own home. Could I make out a quick claim deed for my house with my daughter and son's names on it, put it in my safe deposit box and not file it and at my death my children could file it? Then the house would be in their names.

My lawyer says I do not need a will as long as I want everything to be divided between the two children. What do you say?—Ms. C.T.

Have you asked your lawyer about the *quit-* (not *quick*) claim deed? I think you'll find a deed that's simply signed and put away in your safe deposit box doesn't accomplish anything, now or after your death. Better check.

I'm surprised that any lawyer tells anyone a will isn't needed, and I disagree. It's likely that your children wouldn't have any trouble inheriting your estate in equal portions, but leaving a will makes things simpler, and possibly less expensive, for them.

CHANGING THE ZONING

Dear Edith: How do you go about changing a zoning in your area?—Ms. L.C.

To request an exception to zoning regulations for one particular piece of property, you go before your local zoning board. Neighbors will be invited to your hearing, to voice their support or opposition. It's best to have a lawyer help with the process.

You ask for a nonconforming use if you have been using the property in a way that no longer meets new zoning regulations. You ask for a variance if you intend to prove the zoning works a particular hardship on you. A special-use permit is sometimes granted when the proposed use would benefit the public.

Unless you have some grounds like those stated, it can be difficult to obtain an exception. The neighbors' opinions count.

DIFFICULTY PAYING THE MORTGAGE

Dear Edith: We bought our home about three years ago. After making several repairs, we started having difficulty making payments on the mortgage. Checking with the mortgage company they are saying we have six months to a year to come up with the payments. We have checked with a lawyer. He is saying sell the house or go bankrupt. We would like to keep our house. Are there any other alternatives?—Mrs. T.C.

Come up with the payments.

When you don't pay exactly as promised, the lender has the right to force a prompt sale. You're lucky they're offering you beathing space; they don't have to.

Consumer credit counseling can be a great help. The nonprofit agency may have a different name in your city; if you're in a small town, try the phone book for the nearest city. If there's any way to get straightened out, they'll help with the process.

(Beware, though, of rip-off "agencies" that offer to straighten you out for large fees.)

Your lawyer is right. If it turns out you can't get current, you're better off selling the place promptly. Otherwise, you'll only get further in debt, and the legal costs of foreclosure will pile up. As for bankruptcy—follow your attorney's guidance.

SON LIVED IN TENNESSEE

Dear Edith: When the lady next door died, her son came up for the funeral and we bought her house from him the next day "as is," no lawyers, just we gave him a check and he signed a deed. Now we find out the basement is very wet. He lives in Tennessee and doesn't even answer our letters. Do we have a case against him?—Mrs. S.

You're worrying about the wrong thing. When you bought as is, you probably agreed to take on any and all problems. But the big question is, do you really own the place? You don't unless that son owned it and had the right to sell it to you. Have a lawyer track down the ownership problem right away, or you'll only store up trouble for the future.

CAN'T FIND HER DEED

Dear Edith: Since my husband died I cannot find the deed to my home anywhere. I do not know what he did with it. May I ask how I go about getting a new deed to my home? I am sure my children will need it in case anything happens to me.—C.P.

Don't fret. That deed was good for just one purpose—to transfer ownership to your husband and you, years ago. For the next owner, you—or your children—will write a new deed.

If you ever did want a copy, you could request it from the county clerk, who should have it in the public records.

SON BUILT ON HIS LAND

Dear Edith: My son just built a home on a lot I own. He paid for it. My question is: can I have the local tax collector submit the tax bill for that lot in two parts, the bill for the land to me and a separate bill to my son for the house? Since my son owns the house, I would like him to get the income tax deduction for his share of the property taxes. I'm afraid when the next tax bill comes to me it will include both land and building.—Mr. T.P.

Of course it will, because you own both.

The one who owns the land (you) also owns anything permanently attached to it (the house your son built).

The tax bill is only one complication; insurance is another. Your son will probably want to safeguard the investment he's made in someone else's property. The two of you need a lawyer, for help in straightening things out.

CANCELING THE LISTING

Dear Edith: I have a six-month listing to sell my house. How can I legally get out of this contract now and take out a contract with a better broker? Can I take the house off the market to sell it myself? If I sold to an investor now after the contract is canceled, do I pay a commission?—Mr. K.D.

That could depend on whether the investor saw the house while it was listed, and on the wording of your listing contract.

In most states an owner who is acting in good faith has the right to cancel a listing agreement at any time. The broker may have the right to be reimbursed for time and money expended—advertising, for example.

But if you cancel because you want to sell to someone who has already seen the place, then you're not acting in good faith. In addition, the listing contract you signed probably has a provision to cover such a happening.

CABIN IN CANADA

Dear Edith: My parents inherited a cabin in Canada ten years ago. It is worth about $12,000. They have now given the cabin to my husband and myself. We have paid the taxes and expenses for a year. We would like to know how to go about putting the cabin in our names. Can we do this without a lawyer? What is the least expensive way to handle this?—N.J.

If your parents haven't given you a deed, they haven't given you the cabin. A lawyer in Canada should draw up the document, signed by your parents, which transfers ownership. The deed should then be entered in the public records up there. The process need not be expensive.

TREES IN A LINE

Dear Edith: Please advise if a line of trees (pine) can be placed on a line. —Ms. P.L.

Your neighbors would have the right to remove any part of your trees that went over onto their land, so it's prudent to plant your trees somewhat in from the boundary line.

WHAT HAPPENS WITH FORECLOSURE?

Dear Edith: We are having our house foreclosed and I don't really understand what is happening. Approximately how much money will it cost us when this is all over? Our loan balance is $35,850. And what effect will it have on our credit when we want to purchase another house?—Mrs. T.H.

Disastrous.

Once you've had a foreclosure, it's very difficult ever to place a mortgage with a lending institution again.

What's happening is this: Your house will be sold at auction, with the proceeds going to pay off your loan, back payments, any back taxes, other liens and the legal costs of foreclosure. If there's anything left over, it goes to you. If the place doesn't bring enough, on the other hand, you could have a judgment against you for the shortfall. So the question of how you'll come out depends on the value of the property.

If the place is worth more than the balance on the loan plus all those other amounts, find out if you still have time to sell it. You'd be much better off that way, putting it on the market at a rock-bottom price for a quick deal. Then you wouldn't have that foreclosure on your record.

A lawyer or a broker could investigate for you, but you'd have to act quickly. It may already be too late to stop the process.

LOST THE ABSTRACT

Dear Edith: We made the final payment on our mortgage in November 1984. Our lawyer notified the parties who held the mortgage to forward the abstract to him. Up to now they have not been able to find it; I know they have tried. Our lawyer is out of town so we are not able to talk with him. If we decided to sell the house, would we have a problem?—Mrs. V.J.

The problem comes down to a matter of money.

If you sold, you'd be asked to furnish the abstract (a history of past transactions on the property, taken from the public records). Ordering a new one would cost you several hundred dollars more than simply updating the old one.

BOUGHT ON A LAND CONTRACT

Dear Edith: We have about two more payments and our small farm of sixteen acres will be paid for. We bought it on a land contract for deed in 1962. Is there anything we must do before finishing paying for it?—Mrs. F.P.

Congratulations on making it through to the end of your contract. You must be feeling pretty good.

Go to a lawyer immediately—one who is experienced in real estate matters—and do it before you make that last payment. It's important that the paperwork be handled properly at this point.

MOTHER'S LIFE ESTATE

Dear Edith: My mother says she signed her home over to me yet the tax bill has her name and the words "life estate" and then my name. Could you explain this to me?—Mrs. S.F.

"Life estate" usually means that the house belongs to your mother as long as she lives, and on her death automatically becomes yours (no matter what else her will might say). Meanwhile, your claim on the house is legally known as that of a remainderman—or, given the way things go these days, perhaps it's "remainderperson."

WANTS TO CASH OUT

Dear Edith: Three years ago my boyfriend and I bought a house.

Well, I think it's time for me to separate from him and move out. He refuses to cash me out on my down payment and he refuses to sell the home for he wants to continue living in it.

Could he end up selling without me knowing it? Doesn't he need my signature in order to sell? Also, he's the main name used for the mortgage application, but we are still both on the title.—N.V.

You have the legal remedy called right of partition; you can ask a judge to order the property sold and proceeds divided. At the price level mentioned elsewhere in your letter, though, it's not worth the legal costs of a forced sale, which often fails to bring full price.

If you did it, you might end up losing money. But perhaps a letter from a lawyer, saying you are considering using that right of partition, would convince your friend to pay off your share.

By the way, if you're on the title (one of the owners) then you are also on the mortgage (one of the debtors).

WOULD STILL OWE THE MONEY

Dear Edith: I would like to know if I would be responsible for paying off the remainder of my mortgage balance of $8,000 on my house? I called the real estate department of my mortgage company and they said I would be responsible for the remaining balance even if I decided not to pay for the next three months (the time they'd allow me to live in the house).

It's a 30-year mortgage and I lived here for 22 years but it's falling apart and I don't earn enough to hardly pay the mortgage let alone repairs. I have been suffering with hypertension and worried sick. Please tell me what I can do with this house. —Mr. H.C.

You once promised to pay back that money and you are still responsible for the debt no matter what.

If you are willing to give up the house, why not put it on the market? Surely someone will buy it for more than the $8,000 you owe, and you'll come out with some cash.

KEEPING THE VA LOAN

Dear Edith: We are getting a divorce. We have a VA loan at 9.5 percent. My husband wants to use VA over again where he is living now, so he wants me to buy him out with a new mortgage on my own. I do not want to refinance because I could not qualify alone. So he wants $10,000 instead for the use of the loan.

My lawyers say it is not worth anything so we are at a stalemate. Is there a mortgage out there that I should be looking for to ease my problems? —R.L.

A fixed-rate 9.5 percent is pretty good, and of course if you took out a new loan you'd have substantial closing costs—and that's without the problem of qualifying. Keeping the mortgage you have now is certainly best for you.

But asking a settlement in return for letting you keep it—this is the first time I've heard that one. You might just as logically offer to release that VA entitlement if *he* pays *you* $10,000.

NEIGHBOR MOVED THE STAKE

Dear Edith: My neighbor, a young and impetuous man with little knowlege of the real world, removed my boundary stake so he could "mow his lawn easier." He admits he did it, and I believe it was without malice, just his lack of knowlege. We have no argument about the boundary.

I want him to replace the stake (with a survey). He refuses, and I find it necessary to take him to small claims court to sue for a survey to replace it.

My question (finally) is this: in what part of the law can I find the statutes relating to the placement or removal of property markers? I realize you are not able to offer legal advice, but what might you do if faced with a situation like this? —Mr. K.E.I.

It's common knowlege that God will strike a person dead who moves a surveyor's mark, but I can't quote you chapter and verse.

If you do want to try small claims court, you could have a single interview with an attorney first, to ask just what the statutes in your state say.

CHAPTER AND VERSE

After that item appeared, another reader, a surveyor, sent in chapter and verse: Deuteronomy 19:14 "Thou shalt not remove thy neighbor's landmark...." and 27:17 "Cursed be he that removeth his neighbor's landmark. And all the people shall say, Amen." He suggested a look also at Proverbs 22:28 and 23:10.

WHAT TO DO WITH DEED

Dear Edith: What should I do concerning a deed that I have but the property has been sold some years ago? My husband bought it (I don't know if he got the deed at buying time or after it was paid up) but when he sold it, I found the deed and asked him to give it to the new owners, or to the company he originally bought it from, but he said no. He died a few years ago but I still don't know what to do about the deed since the property does not belong to me. —Mrs. H.D.

A deed is a one-shot affair. It has just a single job: transferring ownership one time. When that act is over a deed is of no further use. Your husband sold by signing a new deed.

My lawyer says that after the transfer, and after the deed's been copied into the public records, one could just as well tear it up and throw it into a wastebasket. Since this old one worries you, perhaps you should do just that.

QUIT-CLAIM DEED

Dear Edith: Will you please advise as soon as possible what is meant by the term "quick claim deed." I've heard it mentioned in a recent death of a friend. —T.K.

A *quit*-claim deed (not *quick*) is a simple document used in real estate to turn over one person's interest (ownership, if any) to another. It is often used in transfers within a family, or to clear up conflicting or vague claims of ownership.

If the first person (grantor) is complete legal owner, then the recipient of the deed (grantee) is complete owner afterwards. If the grantor doesn't really own the property or any part of it, the grantee doesn't actually receive anything and would have no legal recourse. That's because the person signing a quit-claim deed makes no claim that he or she owned the real estate in the first place.

UNHAPPY WITH TITLE INSURANCE

Dear Edith: I purchased a parcel of land and instead of getting an abstract the seller furnished title insurance. I had a lawyer draw up the papers and he seemed to think it was okay but I am from the old school and would rather have an abstract. Is title insurance the way to go in these modern times or would I be better off to get an abstract made up?—Mr. H.F.W.

Yes, these days title insurance is being used instead of abstracts. It's just as valid, legally, and actually a bit safer. But we have lost something—abstracts furnished fascinating reading about the history of the land.

The title insurance promises that you won't suffer from any challenge to your ownership, so there's no need for the expense of an abstract—which doesn't really guarantee anything without a lawyer's opinion anyhow.

WHAT LAWYERS CHARGE

Dear Edith: We plan on selling our home ourselves. We would like to hire a real estate attorney, instead of a real estate agency. Could you give us an idea of how much a real estate attorney usually charges?—Mr. and Mrs. T.L.

Some attorneys ask a flat fee to handle a sale, some charge by the hour, some base their fee on sale price. Locate a couple of lawyers who specialize in real estate, call up their offices, and don't be afraid to ask how you'd be billed.

If the lawyer is going to spend time teaching you how to sell the house and guiding you all along the way, I expect he or she would charge more than if you were using a broker, or if you already knew how to do it on your own.

WHEN PROPERTY TRANSFERS

Dear Edith: At what point during the real estate closing procedure does the property actually change hands? Is it the recording of the deed, or the exchange of funds, or some other parts of the closing process?—R.N.K.

How about a little history here? In the Middle Ages, when few people beyond the clergy were literate, transfer of ownership took place this way: Buyer and seller walked the boundaries of the parcel that was changing hands. Then the seller bent down, picked up a clod of earth and handed it to the buyer. That clod, which actually did change hands, represented the whole field, and the buyer became owner at the moment when he seized it. (The legal term reflecting that old custom still says an owner is "seized of the property.")

Nowadays a written deed is used instead of the clod of earth, and the property is transferred at the exact moment when the document is put into the hands of the buyer—or, particularly in areas where closings are held in escrow, in the hands of someone designated by the buyer to receive it.

LANDLORD'S HANKY-PANKY

Dear Edith: Our landlord wants us to buy this house, get an assumable loan, then sell it back to him, so he can get his cash out of it. He says he will pay all costs and give us $2,000 when it's all over. Is this legal? If legal, is it moral? If legal and moral, is it a good idea?—Mr. E.T.

And the answers are: probably not, probably not and probably not.

It sounds as if your landlord wants to use you as a front to acquire a valuable low-down-payment FHA loan, which requires you to sign a statement that you are buying the house for your own use. You'd be committing perjury, a serious legal offense. And after you deeded the house back to him, you'd still be personally responsible for the loan for at least five years.

Your landlord may not realize there are new rules about assumptions of FHA loans. To take over your loan that soon, he'd have to go in and prove financial capability to the bank. The requirement was put in to stop abuses.

Ask your landlord to put his proposal in writing so you can have a lawyer explain it. My guess is that you won't hear any more about the matter.

GOING BACK TO MOTHER

Dear Edith: I have lost my job and my marriage and will be moving in with my mother in another state. Is it really legal for her community to restrict residents to over age 55? Today with so many grown children coming home because living alone is so very costly, this ruling seems unbelievable.—Ms. S.R.

It's probably legal, though. Housing discrimination on the basis of age is allowed in certain developments that meet federal guidelines.

Age discrimination in housing is illegal in many states, but again the law usually allows exceptions for senior citizen developments. Your mother knew the rules when she bought there; it may have been one of the attractions for her.

OBJECTS TO WORDING

Dear Edith: I recently came across a leaflet called "Show and Sell" by Edith Lank. I would like to copy it and hand it out because the article has considerable value for potential clients who want to prepare their homes for the market. But I hesitate to do so because it refers to the agent throughout as "she." I have highlighted the "hers" and "shes" in the enclosed copy of the article.

In this predominantly female world of real estate there are some males. I resent the suggestion the leaflet seems to make to "hire a female broker."—Mr. D.K.

Now you know how the other half lives.

I find "he or she" irritating, so if I'm using just one pronoun, sometimes it'll be one, sometimes the other. I would point out that the leaflet costs $1 and is copyrighted, which makes photocopying it illegal.

FINDING A LAWYER

Dear Edith: How do I go about locating a real estate lawyer? How do I find one who specializes and is familiar with buys and sells?—Mr. T.O.

Real estate brokers know which local attorneys specialize in real property work. They have opinions on which are the better ones, too. Some agents prefer to mention several lawyers' names rather than specifically recommending one. Call a couple of real estate firms and ask the managing brokers for suggestions.

You can also call a bank's mortgage department and ask what firm (in a small town, what specific lawyer) handles its own real estate work. If you call a large law firm, ask to be directed to its real estate specialist.

I don't have much faith in the standard advice "Ask your local Bar Association" because you may simply receive whatever name is next at the top of the list.

NEVER GOT A TAX BILL

Dear Edith: We bought a lot in another area, and while we were paying for it (five years) the developer paid the property taxes. After that we never received a tax bill, though it would have been simple for them to find out our address. If we had received a bill we would have paid it.

Now we suddenly find our lot is being sold for unpaid taxes, and we can't get it back without paying almost three thousand dollars. This seems so unfair. I would like to know what recourse I have.—Mr. L.T.

I'm afraid you were liable for property taxes even if you didn't receive a bill. Just bite the bullet and pay up.

MENTIONED IN WILL

Dear Edith: I own a house and wonder if I'd have trouble selling it. You see it is mentioned in my will. Maybe that's why my daughter-in-law thinks that I can't. She told me to "just try and sell it." I think the will part is what swayed her into thinking that I can't. What is your opinion?—Mrs. K.T.

10/28/92

VA CHANGES

A loan Guaranty Letter 26-92-15 sets out major changes to VA loan programs. The biggest change is the replacement of a VA-established rate with a negotiated rate. <u>Loans already locked in are not affected by these changes as they fall under the old rules</u>.

Brief summary:

<u>VA will no longer set a rate</u>; the rate is negotiable between buyer and seller (same as FHA).

<u>Discount Points</u> may be paid by the Veteran, but points cannot be financed.

<u>Refinances for rate reduction</u>:

1) Points cannot be financed.

2) Funding fee is reduced to .5 of the loan amount.

<u>Veteran-paid discount points</u> (other than Interest Rate Reduction): If points increase <u>any amount</u> over that shown on the final application, lender must verify sufficient funds. Changes to application must be initialed and dated by Veteran.

<u>Increase in rate</u>: If rate increases more than 1% over the rate on the final application, the loan must be re-underwritten. Changes to application must be initialed and dated by Veteran.

<u>Reservists/National Guard</u>: Subject to certain criteria, reservists and National Guard members are now eligible for VA loans; the funding fee is computed on a higher schedule, ranging from 1.25 to 2%, depending on down payment.

People mentioned in your will don't have any claim on your property until you die. Meanwhile, you have every right to sell the house, unless something else is involved.

There's the off chance, for example, that you inherited the place with only a life tenancy. In that case, your son might automatically become owner when you died. Even so you could theoretically sell, if you could find anyone willing to buy with that provision.

ESTABLISHING OWNERSHIP

Dear Edith: I plan to use the money from the sale of our home to subcontract and build a new home. When you complete the home how do you establish ownership or deed if you don't go through a lending institution for a mortgage?—Mr. V.V.

Getting a mortgage loan doesn't help you establish ownership. If you have a deed to the lot you build on, that's all you need. When you own the land, you own anything later built on it.

FENCE INSIDE THE LINE

Dear Edith: To keep my horses in I needed a fence. Due to the nature of the land I had to put the fence several feet inside the surveyed property line. A neighbor said I will lose the land on the other side of the fence as I have established a new property line. Is this the case?—Mr. K.O.

Putting up a fence does not establish a property line. If your neighbor on the other side used your land (to garden, for example) and you took no notice of it, then after a period of years you might be in danger of losing that strip. A lawyer could help head that off with some simple paperwork.

LETTERS I DIDN'T PRINT

Dear Edith: . . . being on the sunset side of life I have to look ahead and make my own provisions. But I'm in a quandary, and have been taken to the cleaners financially three times by men, so until I find a reputable female attorney don't tell me to see a lawyer. Delighted to see on TV you were a woman as opposed to a man.

Dear Edith: I got married December 6. My husband bought a home but he didn't put my name on it, just his. He bought it after we got married. Is there any legally way I can get my name on the deed? P.S. I didn't move in the house with him because of that. Answer urgent needed.

PART 3

Selling a Home

"Is the statue to be buried upside down?"

Nineteen semesters now, I've taught college real estate courses—and I still have things to learn from my students.

One evening the subject was listing property to sell, and one couple spoke up.

"We've just heard about the service this one agency performs in Chicago. When they list your house, they bury a small statue of St. Joseph in the backyard, upside down, facing the house, to ensure the sale."

"Someone's pulling your leg," I was sure.

"Not a bit," said another student. "I've heard that—they do it in Los Angeles."

"What do you mean, Los Angeles?" said a woman in the front row. "I had this friend, had a landmark house near here, big historic thing, hard to find the right buyer, and she buried a St. Joseph in the backyard, but she said it had to be in the far right-hand corner."

"My father-in-law was a builder," contributed one woman. "And every time, before he started a house, he made a novena to St. Joseph."

St. Joseph was, after all, a carpenter, and I can see doing better work after invoking his aid. But an upside-down statue? For a sale?

We took a survey. About 5 percent of the students had heard of the practice, which seems to cut across ethnic lines. The technique mentioned is remarkably uniform and always involves burying the saint on his head, facing the house. One woman had done it herself, but "I put the statue in a little cardboard box, with cotton wool, before I buried it."

Next morning, I called the manager of a store that sells religious items.

"Don't use my name," she said, "Sure we carry them. People don't usually say why they buy, so I don't know for sure. But quite often someone comes in and says her husband was just transferred out of town and she needs a statue of St. Joseph."

"I gave a St. Joseph medal to an aunt of mine as a joke—we were just kidding. She hung it out on a tree and immediately a man came to the door and asked if she'd ever considered selling her property. She called me up right away and said I shouldn't fool around with it."

The practice has evidently found its way into literature—the nuns in the novel "Lilies of the Field" buried a St. Joseph when they needed a parcel of real estate for their chapel.

In the book, it worked.

In the column, it was a big mistake. I never should have mentioned it in public, for the letters came in over the next couple of years. I swore never to bring it up again, so these became more...

LETTERS I DIDN'T PRINT

Dear Edith: In December my husband and I moved into our home. A friend came over with his dog and the dog dug up a religious statue in our front yard. I remember reading something about it, but can't get what to do straight. Is it for the seller, for good luck selling the home? Or is it just for good luck for whomever is living in the home. Should we put it back? If so, is it to be buried upside down? This matter is really bothering us. Please respond.—P. and L.H.

Dear Edith: After reading your column concerning enlisting the help of St. Joseph in selling a home, I proceeded to follow your directions. We had not had one offer on our house which had been listed for five months. Needless to say, one month later we had three good offers come in on the same evening. Was it our broker (we did change companies) or St. Joseph? I'm not going to speculate.

My question is when to remove the statue from the ground? Or is it to remain buried?—B.B.

My guess is that they also dropped their asking price. But enough of that. Now to the serious business of selling.

CHAPTER 12

Selling Basics

DOING ONLY ONE THING WRONG

Dear Edith: I'm going to put my house up for sale, have recently been widowed and have never taken care of any business deals. I want to sell it myself and just get a lawyer for the closing. I still owe $12,000 to my mortgage company. Should I pay that off now or when I sell? It was a fixed rate mortgage from the VA. Do I need the buyer to sign something, I don't know what it's called but I understand that if they don't the house could come back to me?

Who pays for title insurance? Also on the mortgage it mentions a stove, hood and refrigerator. They wore out long ago. Must I leave the replacement items with the house? We bought the house for $22,500 in 1968. In recent years we did all the following work....I would like to ask $70,000. Does that sound unreasonably high to you? Please give me all the help you can. I'm afraid I'm doing all the wrong things.—Mrs. D.C.

You're doing only one thing wrong, but it's a big one.

I've never said everyone should use a real estate agent, but Mrs. C., you should. The jungle is just full of lions waiting to pounce on unprotected lambs like you. I'm referring not to real estate brokers, but to would-be investors who have been coached by those TV gurus about how to take advantage of innocent sellers.

I haven't the slightest idea how much your house should sell for—and neither do you. You need a careful analysis of recent nearby sales, done by a neighborhood broker.

As for your other questions: You pay off your mortgage when you sell; it isn't likely a buyer will assume such a small one. Sometimes the seller pays for title insurance; more often the buyer does; sometimes none is used. You needn't leave appliances.

I can only guess how many other things you don't know. Really, you should talk with agents. I'll bet your lawyer would agree.

DOLLING UP THE HOUSE

Dear Edith: Is there some guideline on how much we should spend in getting our house ready for the market? I know condition helps a great deal, right? Would there be a dollar amount, or a percentage of listing price?—Mrs. P.E.

The principal guideline is to put in as much soap, water and elbow grease as possible, and as little cash as possible. Most of the things that show your house to best advantage cost nothing but effort.

Just working on the outside, tidy walks and lawns, keep your garage door closed, move out old cars or RVs, take down strings of Christmas lights, clear the lawn of toys and moldy shopping guides. On porch or patio you tidy furniture, remove muddy paw prints, polish brass on the door, replace a burnt-out light bulb or worn doormat, tighten loose house numerals, and perhaps freshen the threshold with a bit of black paint.

All your windows should be sparkling clean, all your closets tidy so they look larger. As for any cash outlay: An experienced real estate broker can look over the place and advise you whether it pays to invest real money anywhere.

SELLING FOR QUICK CASH

Dear Edith: I see several ads from realty companies who will buy your house for cash outright. Is there ever a situation where this could be a good deal, or is it always best to stay away from this?—Ms. D.

Those who buy for immediate cash give you a wholesale price. They will have many expenses before they fix the place up and sell it on the open market.

Your house is worth more at retail, to some one who is going to live in it. The quick-cash sale is necessary in some circumstances, but not if the house is in fairly good shape and if you have the time to put it on the market and wait for the right buyer.

NEGOTIATING COMMISSIONS

Dear Edith: Is it possible to negotiate about the broker's fee, or even pay a flat fee regardless of the sale price?—Ms. T.C.

Yes, broker's commissions are negotiable, and flat fees are possible. Whether any particular broker wants to negotiate is of course a different matter.

Remember that the agent who agrees to an unusually low fee may have to limit some services. You'd want to inquire particularly about advertising, which is the broker's single largest expense.

NOT A FREE APPRAISAL

Dear Edith: A real estate appraisal outfit wants $250 to tell me how much my house is worth. A real estate agency said they would do it for free. Which one would furnish me with the more realistic figure? — Mr. T.A.

You have a good question there.

What is the purpose of the appraisal? A detailed written report by a qualified appraiser is probably more accurate, and is the only kind that could be used in court (inheritance, divorce, arguing with the government, etc.). Just the same, a skilled estimate by a broker familiar with real estate sales in your neighborhood can often be close to eventual selling price.

Real estate etiquette, by the way, frowns on calling anything a "free appraisal." Appraisers hold that if it's free, it's not an appraisal. Instead, you'll find terms like "free market analysis" or "free estimate of value."

DIFFERING OPINION

Dear Edith: After reading your answer to Ms. F.S., I wanted you to know I believe any intelligent person who does his/her homework can sell their house with a real estate broker not in the picture. — P.M.S.

In the item you refer to, I had pointed out possible pitfalls because that's what F.S. had asked about. I did say that some home sellers do manage on their own — but they're usually financially and legally sophisticated persons who are willing, as you say, to put in some work.

INFLATING FOR PRIVATE SALE

Dear Edith: How much do you normally inflate your house over market value for a private sale? — Mrs. S.C.

Did you really mean "inflate" or are you asking about discounting your price?

Whether you use a broker or not, you can't raise your price beyond fair market value and still hope to find a buyer. That's because the definition of market value is "what the buying public will offer." People won't pay more when you're selling on your own. On the contrary, because they're making do without a broker's services they will expect some price concession from you and hope to pick up a bargain.

But you wouldn't want to do the extra work yourselves unless you could come out ahead. Ideally, I suppose, you and the buyers would split a saved commission down the middle. Things seldom work out that neatly, of course.

SELLING IN FLORIDA

Dear Edith: We own four lots in Port Charlotte, Florida, that we would like to sell. If these lots were yours, how would you go about selling them?—Mr. P.K.

I'd send for a few copies of the local newspaper, and note which brokers are advertising such lots for sale. Then I'd write, or even better, phone a few of them, and list the property with the one who inspires the most confidence.

SELLING SISTER'S HOME

Dear Edith: We want to sell my sister's home and the real estate agent says it will have to be listed with an FHA or VA loan, nothing down. He says we will have to pay the mortgage points (5 percent), mortgage insurance, house taxes and insurance, credit report, appraisal, title insurance, FHA or VA inspections and lots more.

We are very confused. Are the sellers responsible for all these items if sold with a VA or FHA loan?—Mr. H.T.

No. And even when the seller does agree to bear most of the costs, lenders require the buyer to contribute a certain minimum amount of money.

The agent is describing one sort of sale, to a buyer who has almost no cash. There are plenty of other ways to sell, even a modest house. If that's the only way he's proposed, let me suggest that there are also plenty of other agents. If you haven't already signed a listing contract, find a different broker and make sure it's someone who can explain things so that you'll understand.

LETTING THE LENDER KNOW

Dear Edith: I bought my house a year ago with an adjustable rate mortgage. If I decide to sell my house do I need to call the mortgage holder, or can I wait until and if the house is sold?—Ms. H.O.

You don't need to talk to the bank until your house is sold. At that point the person handling legal aspects of the closing will do it for you.

You might want to find out ahead of time, though, whether your mortgage is assumable and exactly what the terms would be. The information could be valuable to potential buyers.

HOUSE IS FREE AND CLEAR

Dear Edith: I was fortunate enough to be able to pay cash for my house when I bought it a few years ago, and I've heard it would be hard to sell because I do not have a loan out on it. Is this true, and if so, why? Also what do I need to do to be able to sell my home?—Mr. O.Y.

The only time a mortgage helps with the sale of a house is when it's an assumable (FHA or VA) loan high enough to be of value to the next buyer.

The fact that the house is free and clear won't hinder your sale at all. As for what to do to sell your house: Your letter leads me to believe your first step should be to locate a broker who can explain things to your satisfaction, someone you can feel confident with.

DIFFERENT SORTS OF VALUE

Dear Edith: I wanted to place my mother's home on the market. The real estate man gave me a figure. Then the insurance company sent me a bill, insuring the place for $10,000 more than that. I contacted the insurance agent and he said replacement value is different; he wants insurance for 90 percent of replacement value. On my mother's tax bill, though, the value for tax purposes is something else again.

So do I list for sale at 90 percent of replacement cost, the value for tax purposes, estimated market value or what?—Mrs. N.I.O.

Insure for the amount the insurance agent stipulates. Pay taxes on the amount the assessor sets. But list for sale at or near the broker's estimate of market value. That's the best guess at what the buying public will be willing to pay.

SELLING WITH FURNITURE

Dear Edith: Please advise on selling my home furnished. Does that increase or decrease the salability of the house? How much more should we increase the sale price? We will leave draperies, wall-to-wall carpeting, and all furniture.—Mrs. D.K.

Comparatively few buyers will come to look at your completely furnished home. Most people already have furniture or look forward to choosing their own. There could be someone eager for exactly what you have to offer, but the chances are slim. Meanwhile, anything that cuts down on the pool of potential buyers diminishes your chances for top price.

Discuss furniture after you have a firm contract with the buyers. Then, for whatever they don't want, plan on a tag sale or auction, whichever is used in your area.

WANTS MARKET VALUE

Dear Edith: I own a small general store that I want to sell. I have refused three offers to purchase because those offers were grossly insufficient. My problem is I don't know what my store is worth on the market. I must get true market value. How can I find out how much that is?—Mr. K.N.

By paying attention to those three offers. Your store is worth whatever people are ready to pay for it. That statement, in fact, is a thumbnail definition of market value.

SELLING AND BUYING

Dear Edith: My husband and I have two different opinions. He says we must sell our home and then buy the next one. I say you buy a home and then sell yours. Our home is free and clear, and buying another home would be cash. —Mrs. T.E.

Because your next purchase won't depend on a new mortgage, it's best to start by putting your present house on the market first. While you won't require a loan, your buyer might, and that could take three months or so. But as soon as your house is listed for sale, there's no harm in starting your house-hunting.

Real estate brokers are used to handling situations like yours. An agent—and your lawyer—can arrange contracts and dates so the two transactions dovetail. It's done all the time.

BUYING OFF THE EX-WIFE

Dear Edith: I am newly married. My husband and I reside in his home because his children did not want to move, and anyhow, the only offer we received while it was on the market was $8,000 less than we could accept. Meanwhile his ex-wife, who owns a share of the house, wants us to buy her out. She has submitted us with a price she wants (no exceptions) based on the high dollar the real estate company was asking for the house. She won't take the tax assessed value into account at all.

How do we arrive at a fair settlement?—Mrs. T.O.

The tax assessment figure isn't relevant, but neither is the price at which you listed the house. The offer you received just may be the best indication of value.

In divorce situations, a common solution is for each party to pay for a professional appraisal of market value, with an agreement ahead of time to average the two estimates and use that figure for settling up. In some cases, the two appraisers are asked to choose a third one.

CAN'T SELL IN FOUR YEARS

Dear Edith: I am a widow 69 years old. I had to move near my daughter, bought a house here. The problem is I am getting low on money, keeping up my old house in my home town. It takes all my social security for taxes and insurance and leaving fuel on which is draining me.

How can I make money off this house or sell it? I've had it in a real estate agent's hands for four years. Is there any bank or real estate person that would give me a fair price for it?—Mrs. T.W.

Four months—never mind four years—is usually long enough for a thorough test of the market.

Either you have a remakably inept agent, or, more likely, you are holding out for more than the place is worth.

WITHDRAWING IN THE WINTER

Dear Edith: If we place our house on the market in October and it doesn't sell by November, should we take it off until April or keep it on?—Mr. R.

You have nothing to lose by keeping your home on the market through the winter. Although fewer buyers are looking then (except, of course in southern resort areas), those who are house-hunting then mean business.

Unless your house is underpriced, you may be unrealistic in expecting a sale within a few weeks. Sometimes it can take several months to test the market properly.

BUYERS MAKE VALUE

Dear Edith: We're going to be putting our house up for sale. If you bought a house for, say, $80,000 and put in professional landscaping, patio, custom drapes and ceiling fans, total cost $7,000, would the value be $87,000, especially if you're in an affluent suburb?—Mrs. H.A.

If your question refers to probable selling price, you're on the wrong track. Unless you bought the place yesterday, your cost is no guide to today's market value. The house you mention might be worth more than $87,000, or less. The important question is—what have nearby similar properties sold for recently?

Value is established not by the seller, but by the buying public.

SELLER PAYING POINTS

Dear Edith: We are putting our house on the market and our real estate agent was vague about who pays what. I realize that anything can be negotiated, but if the buyer gets an FHA mortgage, does the seller have to pay all the points?—Mrs. C.P.

The VA says the borrower (buyer) can be charged only one point. Any other points must be paid by someone else, usually the seller. With an FHA loan, the question of who pays points may be freely negotiated by buyer and seller along with the sale price.

RESORT LOTS AGAIN

Dear Edith: In 1962 we bought a lot in Arkansas for $2,000. We had it paid for 10 years later and have been paying taxes on it, which now run close to $80 a year. We don't intend to move there or build on it and our children don't want it.

We wrote to a realty firm there and asked them to put it on the market, but they wrote back that they are not selling lots now. Should we hold on to it and continue paying the taxes, or just let it go? We are retiring soon and won't have extra money for the taxes. Any suggestions?—Mrs. S.S.D.

Send for the local paper in the area where the lot is located. Write to every real estate broker who advertises. Explain that you are ready to sell at whatever they'd consider a rock-bottom price. Read the classified ads carefully to see what the lot might be worth, and if no broker wants to handle it, try advertising yourselves, a little below whatever price seems current.

PROPERTY ZONED COMMERCIAL

Dear Edith: We own a block of suburban land, approximately thirty acres, zoned commercial. It has a six-room house on it, and income from billboard rentals.

We have given some thought to putting it on the market. Knowing this would not be a regular house-selling transaction, but rather a commercial sale, what procedures should we follow and what agent do we contact?—Mr. and Mrs. N.O., Jr.

For unusual property like that, the first thing I'd seek would be a paid appraisal—not an agent's simple estimate of value, but a written appraisal by a qualified expert. Look in the yellow pages for real estate appraisers who are members of the leading societies: the American Institute of Real Estate Appraisers, for example, or the Society of Real Estate Appraisers. Call and ask if they consider themselves qualified for your property, and what they'd charge for a market value appraisal.

You are right to seek a specialized sales agent. Read advertisements for commercial real estate, to see which firms handle property like yours; those are the brokers you should contact.

TAKE OUT THAT SINK

Dear Edith: My husband and I purchased this two-family house in 1971. It has separate entrances and exits, water, heating and utilities, and no gutters. The FHA approved it just that way when we bought it.

Now I have a buyer who wants it just as it is, but the FHA insists I remove the second sink and put in gutters. They say because there is no standard size bedroom in the upstairs apartment, I must sell it as a single house. I am selling because of finances. What can I do?—Mrs. P.D.

Your buyer won't be able to get an FHA loan unless the specifications of this new FHA inspection are met.

Probably they won't want the place after the second kitchen has been removed, though. Have you considered taking back the mortgage yourself—lending them the money to buy the place and receiving monthly payments?

If you do, you'll all save something on closing costs. Have your own lawyer check out the buyers' income, debts and credit, however, before you enter into any such arrangement.

DISPUTES ASSESSMENT JUDGMENT

Dear Edith: You wrote "several factors are not relevant to the proper listing price...in many instances, tax assessment figures." I would think for a given location that assessed value would be as good an indicator as any if you have enough sold samples to give a percentage to apply to the subject house's assessed value. Why do you think they are not relevant?—Mr. C.D.

If we could simply say "Every house in this area has gone up by 6 percent in the past year," things would be easy. But one house is beautifully kept, another needs repairs, a third just had a fast-food outlet erected beside it, and a fourth is being sold at a bargain price by a seller who faces foreclosure. Six percent could indeed be the average, and still be wildly off on a particular parcel of real estate.

Tax assessors make a careful, informed effort to estimate market value. So many factors affect individual prices, though, that even experts are sometimes fooled by the reaction of the buying public—which is, in the end, the one thing that determines market value.

TROUBLE WITH HONEST ESTIMATES

Dear Edith: I am a broker and have been in our family real estate business most of my life.

I have to give people estimates on their homes and advice on price. I practically never get a listing because I tell them the truth. They usually sell the house for what I tell them they'll get. Meanwhile other brokers mention a price that sounds so good to the owner, that even though the price is wrong, they get the listing.

I keep thinking I should do the same thing but the people are always so nice I just don't want to pull the wool over their eyes. Home owners should get at least three different opinions from brokers. —Mrs. H.O.S.

And they should ask to see the data that backs up the market analysis. An accurate estimate isn't just pulled out of the air; it's based on research into comparable sales, and an analysis of competing properties.

NO STANDARD COMMISSION

Dear Edith: I am planning to sell my house in the near future and would like to know what is the current commission that is charged by real estate agents. Also, is it necessary to have a "For Sale" sign outside the house?—Mrs. T.M.

How much do doctors charge for office visits? What do photographers want for 8"-by-10" color portraits?

I don't know. I don't know the fees charged by any particular broker, either. To find out, ask them.

You can certainly list with a broker and stipulate that you don't want a lawn sign. Signs do attract interest and help market the property, but it is up to you whether you want one there.

SETTING SEDUCTION SCENE

Dear Edith: At one time you had a recipe for something to use to give a house a pleasant aroma. Would you please tell me what that was?—Mrs. T.W.G.

I may have mentioned that before showing a house, sellers have been known to put gingerbread in the oven, or simmer a bit of vanilla on the stove. Falling in love with a house is like falling in love with a person, and the wise seller sets up a seduction scene that appeals to all five senses.

RESORT LAND AGAIN

Dear Edith: My problem is a building lot in a recreation area. My husband bought it as an investment, assuming it would increase in value. Instead the *value has decreased but the maintenance fee has more than tripled. We paid $3,500 and by now have poured $6,000 into it.*

My husband passed away so now it is my problem. None of my children want this lemon as an inheritance. So far only one of the brokers I wrote to has answered my letter. He thought he might be able to get $3,000 for it. Of course he would require broker's fee etc. out of it. —Mrs. D.T.

Take the money and run. If you wrote to several brokers and only one answered, your impression of the value is probably accurate. Bite the bullet, pay the broker's fees and any legal costs, and get what you can right now.

Land as an investment is a tricky business, and it's not for amateurs. Buying a lot to build on is one thing; holding it for years is, as you've learned, something else.

RUN-DOWN HOUSE

Dear Edith: I live in my mother's house. She lives out of state and we have been talking of selling. The property is in one of the best city neighborhoods. On the other hand, the house is old, run-down and possibly not even structurally sound.

Can you give me some tips on where to begin? If I have it appraised what questions should I ask and if the house is not worth saving, should I get something for it anyhow? Even if they tear it down? Will they even discuss it with me as I will be representing my mother? Should I do repairs before I have it appraised?—Ms. B.J.B.

Even if the house were worthless, the land itself, in a choice neighborhood, would be valuable. Hold off on repairs. Start by calling in local real estate brokers from several different firms, and asking for advice. Most won't charge for the service, and they can judge better than I can through the mail.

Assuming your mother is in agreement with your plans, her being out-of-state shouldn't present many problems. You'll be asked to obtain her signature on various documents, as you get going.

NOT ASSESSED ENOUGH

Dear Edith: We own a one-of-a-kind antique house and are thinking of putting it on the market. It will probably attract a very small segment of the buying public.

We had a market analysis done recently, and the real estate broker suggested we list the house at a figure that is almost twice our tax assessment figure.

Our town is supposed to be at 100 percent assessment. We are concerned that a potential buyer will think our price is way out of line. Should we have the assessor come out and reassess the house so that a higher assessment will appear on the listing?—R.W.

Certainly not.

Few buyers base their offer on your assessment figure. Rather, they decide what the place is worth to them by comparing it with whatever else is on the market. If your tax figure looks low, that can be an attractive extra.

An appraisal, no matter how skillful, is simply an estimate of value. The same goes for your tax assessor's figure. With unique property out in the country, the real estate broker and the assessor could both have trouble finding enough comparable sales to run a proper analysis.

There's no way to tell which came up with the right figure. The only thing that counts is what the buying public will say about the house. You won't find that out until you list the place and test it on the open market.

NOT ONE OFFER

Dear Edith: We listed our house for four months with a local real estate agent and not one offer. Now we have other agents who claim "If we list with them they will sell the house." How can they say that now, when they had a chance before?

We plan to list again in January but don't know what agent to have. Who would you suggest we list with and how should we make sure somebody will make an offer?—Mr. R.E.

When a house doesn't sell after four months, the problem is almost always price.

Did your previous broker suggest lowering your listing price? If so, you were receiving proper advice, and it would be right to give that firm, which has already invested time and advertising expense, another chance.

If your former broker didn't try to get your price reduced, you weren't getting good service. This time, choose the broker who stresses the importance of proper pricing, rather than an agent who promises you the moon.

THAT COSTLY HANDRAIL

Dear Edith: We are selling our home, and the bank's appraiser said we needed a handrail to the basement stairs, which we installed at a cost of $20. Now they say we are to pay a $40 fee in order for the appraiser to come back and verify that it was installed.

This makes it a costly handrail. Why can't the broker just verify that it is there?—Mrs. S.S.

If certain repairs are a condition of a new mortgage loan, the lender is supposed to make an official reinspection to verify that the work has been done. Sometimes they bend a little when it's a minor matter, but if they won't, they won't. No verification, no loan. No loan and your buyers can't buy. That's just the way it is.

HOME IMPOSSIBLE TO SELL

Dear Edith: My unoccupied house is in a high crime area and impossible to sell. I received a violation tag for not painting my garage. When I told them I was considering (not definite) donating my $42,000 house to the government, they suspended my fine. I did not sign anything. Care to comment? —Ms. N.L.

Never mind about the fine and donating the house. I'm interested in two of your other statements—that the house is impossible to sell, and that it's worth $42,000.

That's a $42,000 house only if someone is willing to pay $42,000 for it. If it's really impossible to sell, it's a $10 house.

But no property is totally unmarketable. If you put the place on the market for $10, a buyer would come forward. Any real estate will sell if the price is right. And somewhere between $10 and $42,000 is an asking price that will produce a buyer.

ENGINEER'S INSPECTION

Dear Edith: What does an engineer inspect when he looks over a house? The people who have put an offer on my house want to bring an engineer. What is legal for them to check or not check? How far can they go? My house is in great shape, I just don't like the intrusion. —K.W.

When you signed an agreement that the buyers could bring in an engineer, you gave permission for all of the real estate to be inspected: roof, gutters, insulation, heating, plumbing, electrical system, basement, structural stability, the works.

No one will rummage in your desk drawers for private letters, and your personal belongings are safe from scrutiny.

SELLING LAND IN BELLEVILLE

Dear Edith: I have 50 acres of land in Belleville, Ontario, Canada, a quarter mile from Salmon Trout Lake and I would like to sell it.

Would it be better if I listed the property with a Canadian real estate company or a local company here? Also I don't know what land sells for now in Belleville. Is there any way I can get this information?—K.H.

List with a real estate firm up in Belleville. They can tell you about recent sales of nearby land, and advise on the right listing price.

WHO GETS THE $100?

Dear Edith: I foolishly signed a paper to sell my house and have been in trouble ever since. I had lots of trouble with the buyer. After many unpleasant dealings I finally said I didn't want to sell to him. I've never been able to contact the mortgage company so I can't verify if he got his loan or not, which was part of the contract.

Now he says if he doesn't get his $100 deposit back he'll sue me for the deposit and court costs. Meanwhile I lost two other buyers. If he wins the lawsuit can he put a lien against my home?—M.A.

One hundred dollars is too small an amount for you to incur legal costs, and it's hard to believe the other guy will either, for that amount.

But you could go to small claims court and ask for the $100 to be ruled as properly yours. There's only a small fee; you go in yourself and tell your story to a judge.

If they can prove they were turned down for the mortgage, you may lose and you'll have to give up the $100, but that'll be the end of it.

Next time around, do consider using a real estate broker and a lawyer, right from the beginning. From the details I cut out of your long letter, I think you need your own agent, someone to deal with prospective buyers while you stay out of it.

IS COMMISSION NEGOTIABLE?

Dear Edith: My gut feeling is that I want to list my house with a broker rather than wing it on my own since I am a novice in the field. If so do you usually sign a contract and is the commission negotiable?—Mr. S.K.T.

Yes, you will sign a contract authorizing the broker to find a ready, willing and able buyer, and promising to pay a commission if that is accomplished within a stated length of time. Commission rates are not dictated by any governmental or private group; brokers are free to set their own fees and can negotiate if they want to.

WHICH FIRM TO CHOOSE?

Dear Edith: We are considering three different real estate companies. One is asking two percent lower commission than the others. How to choose?—E.V.

The firm that asks a limited commission usually offers limited services. Nothing wrong with that, as long as you understand what's involved and are willing to work with it.

Advertising is a broker's largest expense; be sure to inquire about how much the discount brokerage will do for your house in that respect. And the broker's largest chunk of time is spent showing houses; it may be that the company will merely send qualified buyers over without accompanying them. If there is a strong multiple listing system in your area, I'd strongly recommend you use a brokerage that participates in it, so your house will be available to buyers who are working with many different companies. The larger the pool of potential buyers, the more likely you are to receive full market value for your house.

CHAPTER 13

Those Real Estate Brokers

"Can one be more pregnant than pregnant?"

When I started the column, I wondered what I'd do if I received a flock of complaints about real estate brokers. Would I publish them impartially, even though I still hold my broker's license for old-times' sake, and my husband is a Realtor?

I never had to decide, because remarkably few letters about disappointing brokers ever come in, and I've published almost every one. As I don't mention my husband's firm in the column, though, this note from my own town is another...

LETTER I DIDN'T PRINT

Dear Edith: I would like to know if you are related in any way to Lank Realtors on South Avenue. If you are could you please let me know in your next column and then I will let you know what my problem is. I wish to remain unknown. Thank you — Unknown

And as there was no return address, I never did find out what that was about.

MORE PREGNANT

Dear Edith:...I was intrigued by your comment that "Realtors subscribe to a code of ethics that goes beyond state regulations for their industry." In my opinion when I am licensed as a broker by the New Jersey Real Estate Commission I am deemed to possess all the ethics necessary to serve the public. How is it possible that by becoming a Realtor I am now more ethical than ethical? Can one be more pregnant than pregnant?

AGENT PAYING THE REST

Dear Edith: When we were selling our house, we had a hard time to get what we wanted for it. So the real estate woman came to us and said these folks will pay only so much, and I will pay the rest. So she put up the final $500 to make the deal. The family that bought the house do not know of this, nor does she want us to say anything to anyone else. Is this legal? We are surprised. —T.L.

In effect, your real estate agent is lowering her commission by $500 and charging you that much less. She does not want people to know about it, so let's not publicize the matter.

Commission rates aren't set by law; they can be negotiated between seller and broker and they can be kept confidential.

HOW LONG TO LIST

Dear Edith: Does one have to list for six months when agents are very persistent about it? Most of them belong to Multiple Listings—is there such a law?—D.N.

You are in complete control of your real estate, and you can authorize an agent to offer it for sale for as short or long a time as you choose. Sellers have been known to give a half-day listing to a single broker: "Well, bring your prospects over this afternoon, and if they buy, we'll pay a commission."

But multiple listing will give your property the best exposure in the market, and most multiple listing systems do require enough time to distribute information about your house to all their members. I can't imagine, though, that they'd require six months.

LISTING WITH THREE BROKERS

Dear Edith: I am going to put my house on the market and would like to know if it is advisable to place the listing with at least three brokers or list with one broker exclusively. —Mr. V.I.

If there is an active multiple listing system in your area, pick one broker who participates in it. Information on your property will then be distributed to all members, and any who want to can act as your agents.

If no multiple listing system is available, ask whether the one agent you want to list with will send out information to other local firms and cooperate with them on your sale.

As for listing with several agents: If you do, make sure the contracts you sign are what is known as "open" listings, which promise to pay commission only to the broker who brings you an acceptable offer. Otherwise, you could end up liable for several commissions.

TOO MANY FRIENDS

Dear Edith: I own four pieces of property. I plan to put them on the market within the next few months. I have three friends, all of whom sell real estate. They each have hinted that they expect me to list the properties with them.

I would like to give all of them a chance to sell the properties, but how do you split four properties among three people? Because the value of each one differs, how do I decide who gets what property to sell?—Mr. E.J.

Why not be frank with your friends, and tell them just what you told me?

Invite them all to a listing luncheon, where they can cut cards or wrist-wrestle. The winner may choose to handle either the most valuable parcel, or the two least expensive; there's no predicting which a given agent might prefer. Your second friend then chooses, and the one with the short straw gets to list what's left.

FRIENDS DRAWING STRAWS

Dear Edith: Shame on you for the advice to the man who wanted to list four properties for sale, and had three friends in the business. (You advised them to draw straws.)

Although it is good to have friends in the real estate business, selling a home is, in fact, business and should not be treated as a social event. Professional real estate people pride themselves on delivering results because of their expertise and knowledge, not just because of social contacts.

Performance and compentency should be the determining factor, not random drawing of straws.—E.R.

I'm sure you're right, but if you remember, the reader didn't ask how to find the most expert broker. He already knew he wanted to share his four listings among three friends, and obviously wanted to retain the friendships.

JUST SEND A CLIENT

Dear Edith: I recently purchased a home which was for sale by the owner. A real estate agent helped throughout the process, knowing full well that no commission would be involved. Is there a proper way to say thank you to the agent for the time and trouble?—D.F.

Money is always acceptable. Only a broker may receive money from the public, so direct your gift to the managing or principal broker in the office, who will channel it to that agent. Enclose a letter of appreciation, which will probably be posted on the office bulletin board.

Less gratifying, but always pleasant, are plants, flowers, gift certificates or a dinner invitation. Most real estate agents, though, if asked "How can I ever thank you?" would reply "Just recommend me to someone else."

BUYERS IN A HURRY

Dear Edith: Do you believe the buyer who is in a hurry to look at something is not a serious buyer? It seems to me that a sincere buyer will plan to spend time with you and not be last minute in his/her approach. —Ms. R.B., licensed sales associate.

My guess is that you haven't been in real estate long. Perhaps you had a bad experience with inconsiderate buyers.

As a broker, though, I'd much prefer to work with buyers who want immediate attention, rather than ones who plan to go out next Sunday afternoon if the weather's good. The typical agent enjoys prospects who are in a hurry. They are likely to be people who have a housing problem and need to solve it soon. They represent a good investment of time and effort.

THAT MICROWAVE OVEN

Dear Edith: I recently sold a home in Pennsylvania. The agent promised to pay me $300 upon closing of my house. The amount represented part of the cost of a year-old microwave oven the buyer insisted should be included in the sale.

Upon closing the broker refused to pay me the agreed-upon amount. I thought she was honorable and never asked for a written agreement. What can I do? Morally and monetarily I can't let her get away with this. —Mrs. L.

In most states the law does not allow a real estate salesperson or broker to share a commission with any unlicensed person, not even with the buyer or seller. Strictly speaking, the agent may not have had any right to offer you the $300, which could be construed as an illegal kickback. Such arrangements do occur, though, when an agent tries to save a complicated transaction.

Complain first to the agent's managing broker, the person in charge of her office. Contact the local Board of Realtors, if her firm belongs.

You might also take her into small claims court, which you can do at little cost without an attorney. You might not win, but you'd have the satisfaction of hearing a judge's opinion in the matter.

BROKER'S FLAT FEE

Dear Edith: Some time ago I read that a person selling his house can talk to a real estate person and arrange to pay him $500 instead of the commission brokers usually get. Of course the seller has to do a few things himself. Would you know whether this is true or not? And what the seller has to do himself?—Mr. D.M.

I can't speak for other brokers. To find out if they'd take a flat fee for limited services, ask them.

I can make some guesses about what would and wouldn't be involved. For such a fee, a broker could not afford to pay for much advertising, or spend time showing your house to prospective buyers. You'd probably be asked to do those things yourself.

It's likely a broker would look over the property and give you advice on pricing, furnish lawn signs, handle phone calls and screen prospects, send buyers over to look at the property, negotiate an agreement and give the buyer advice on how to obtain financing. Following through on the mortgage application might or might not be included; it can be time-consuming.

There'd be no point in entering such a listing in the multiple listing system, because other firms would have no incentive to bring their buyers to your property.

FROM A SECRETARY

Dear Edith: I am a real estate secretary, and I wish you would explain to people who call up that I'm not allowed to give information on houses for sale. Sometimes they get upset and think I'm putting them off.—Mrs. R.C.

Perhaps the public doesn't realize that you would need a license to participate in the sale of real estate. You may not perform any of a salesperson's functions. The managing broker who allowed you to take an active part in the firm's sales effort would also be violating license law.

You are acting properly when you limit your service to taking messages and forwarding them to agents. Since you haven't seen the houses listed with your firm, answering questions about them wouldn't do justice to either sellers or buyers.

AVOIDING VICIOUS NEIGHBOR

Dear Edith: I need to sell my house because of my vicious neighbor. Unfortunately, he owns a real estate agency and it would just kill me to have him sell my house and so make a profit from my family.

I can't list on multiple listing service because then I would be legally forced to let him or his agents enter my home and that would just eat away at me.

But if I give another agency the exclusive right to sell can I say that they can cooperate with other companies but not with my neighbor's agency?—Mrs. G.A.

You run a risk, if you limit the showing of your property to certain buyers or to certain agents. You might be accused of illegal discrimination—on racial or religious grounds, for example. Such a charge could land you in serious trouble.

Of course that's not what you have in mind at all. But such accusations are easy to make and difficult to disprove. If your neighbor is vicious, as you say, he might try for trouble along those lines.

Discuss the situation with a lawyer before taking any steps to sell.

AVOIDING THE COMMISSION

Dear Edith: I am interested in buying a restaurant and a home, maybe together. How long after a broker shows commercial or residential property is there no longer a legal obligation by the seller or potential buyer to pay a commission to the broker?—Mr. V.C.

The answer depends on the terms of the original listing contract signed by the seller, or the buyer's broker agreement (if there was one) signed by the buyer. Consult a lawyer before taking any action.

COMPETING WITH HER AGENT

Dear Edith: I want to put my house on the market and understand that if I list with a broker I can also put in the agreement that I have the option to sell on my own as well. If so, must I advertise at the broker's price or may I sell lower? Are there limits or conditions set on my own advertising, open houses etc.?—Mrs. F.I.

If a broker said you could sell on your own without paying a commission, you must ask that broker the questions you're asking me. It would all depend on the particular listing contract you signed. What you describe is a form of open or exclusive agency listing.

With such a listing, you'd be free to advertise, hold open houses and set any different price you wanted, but again, exact terms would be set out in the contract.

If there is a strong multiple listing system in your area, I'd recommend using a broker who participates in it, because it's to your benefit to have many local firms working on your house. And most multiple listing systems will handle only exclusive right-to-sell listings, under which you give up your right to remain in competition with them.

CHAPTER 14

Real Estate as a Career

"Our son didn't receive anything."

Jack Smith, the columnist, voiced some irritation with people who say that when they retire they'll "do some writing." He resented the assumption that because it sounds simple, writing for publication can be done by just about anyone.

In the same way I resent people who believe that anyone who knows the subject can stand up before a class and teach. (Just try it!) And it's particularly irritating to discover how many people think that someday they'll dabble in "selling a little real estate."

Most people assume that selling real estate involves finding someone who wants to buy a house—but that's no challenge at all, that's easy. It's the smallest part of the job, just the tip of the iceberg. Making sure the would-be buyer is financially capable, following the transaction through to its successful conclusion—that's where skill and knowlege come in.

Real estate is a fascinating field, and many men and women do well in it, but it takes study, long hours and hard work—it can't be done off the top of one's head.

WITHOUT A LICENSE

Dear Edith: I was very involved recently in helping a friend sell his home "for sale by owner." It was a little bit of pain, but the money he saved was well worth it. My question is, what laws restrict me from helping people sell their homes on their own for a small fee?—D.S.

Real estate license laws.

You might as well ask "What laws restrict me from performing unlicensed brain surgery at cut-rate prices?" I suppose it'd be all right until you happened to make a mistake.

Granted, you can't do as much harm as an amateur brain surgeon. But by practicing real estate without training or a license you'd lay your friends open to mistakes, complications and losses, and you'd lay yourself open to lawsuits.

The practice of real estate often involves handling substantial amounts of other people's money. All else aside, that would dictate supervision by the state.

Study, work and earn a broker's license (it sounds as if you'd enjoy the field). Then you can charge fees as small as you wish.

PARENTS ARE GETTING NERVOUS

Dear Edith: Our son, who has recently gone into real estate, had no job at the time and we paid for the test he took and passed which was expensive. Then we paid so much for him to go into Multiply Listing.

Now we are informed he has to pay $35 per month for the Multiply Listing. He spends much time on the floor as they call it and does not receive anything for his time while the others are out showing property and etc. My questions are:

Why doesn't he draw a sum while on floor duty answering phones and etc.? When and how will he begin to bring in money? How does he receive his share of sales and when?

One party working for the same office has just closed a sale and OUR SON DIDN'T RECEIVE ANYTHING. —Mrs. D.H.

I sympathize with your concern, but that's just the way most offices operate. Few real estate salespersons are hired as employees. Traditionally, real estate agents work as independent contractors, sharing with their supervising brokers the commissions on sales they negotiate.

That floor duty gives your son a chance to meet prospective buyers and sellers, and it shouldn't be long before he finds work to do. He'll receive his first check when his first transaction closes; brokers often warn beginners that it may be six months down the line.

SALESMAN AFTER 60

Dear Edith: I am now 63 years of age come next September. Is this a suitable age for a single man with no family to go into real estate sales? I already have a sales license but never used it, have the good fortune to have a local agency hold it for me. Now being retired and already bored I was thinking of going gung ho into the real estate sales field. I am concerned about the age problem. Your opinion would be most appreciated. —Mr. C.R.

Real estate brokerage makes an excellent second career, and you'll be able to work as little or as much as you like. I'll guarantee you won't be bored. Some years ago a retiree came into my husband's firm and sold his first million dollars' worth of real estate within eight months. He's still going strong.

FINDING OUT ABOUT REAL ESTATE

Dear Edith: I'm a recent graduate from high school and I'm interested in a career in real estate, but I do not know if this is what I really want. What do you think of the idea of seeking employment as a secretary in a real estate office?—Ms. N.K.

I think it's a fine idea.

Becoming a licensed salesperson involves formal study, state examination and at least a few months with no money coming in. That's not worth your investment unless you're really interested.

Working as a secretary, on the other hand, means you'd have a salary right from the start. Keep your eyes and ears open in a real estate office for a few months, and you'll soon find out whether or not you want a career in brokerage.

PART-TIMER TROUBLE

Dear Edith: I am qualified for a salesperson's license but find it extremely difficult to enter the field on a part-time basis. Why is this the case?—T.T.

As you know, licensed salespersons are not allowed to practice real estate on their own. You must find a sponsoring broker.

Many firms feel that training part-timers isn't worth their investment of time and effort. And because the broker is legally responsible for a salesperson's actions, brokers worry about taking on someone whom they cannot supervise daily.

Nevertheless, if you look promising it should be possible to locate a broker who will take you on.

WHAT ABOUT CHILD CARE?

Dear Edith: My wife is interested in a real estate career, possibly part-time, but is very concerned about child care and supervision. Our daughter is four. We are worried even beyond the time when she starts school—what about the after-school hours?

How do other mother/real estate agents handle these problems? What about the need to be at the client or buyer's disposal at irregular times and durations?—Mr. G.H.

Many of an agent's irregular hours come evenings and weekends. You'll be able to handle child care for your wife at those times, just as, I assume, she handles it for you while you're at work.

After-school care is often available through local school systems, community organizations, or private arrangements. These days, many two-earner families have faced the problem you raise.

In addition, part-time agents can work in teams, with one covering for the other. In many offices, a cooperative managing broker will step in for an emergency.

CHAPTER 15

Seller Financing

"It's ridiculous to hire an attorney to pay a man $10,000."

Most seller financing goes smoothly. Buyers pay as promised, balloon loans are refinanced in time, everyone is happy—seller-lender, buyer-borrower, and the IRS. But the few deals that go sour are the ones people write to the newspaper about.

LETTER I ALMOST DIDN'T PRINT

Dear Edith: A couple have financed their home and are supposed to pay by the first of every month. The couple says the party receiving the money should date the receipt the same as the check and not the date the check is received. Even their lawyer says that....In my opinion, the lawyer doesn't know much about the business world except to charge a high price. Please tell us who is right....I want this printed in the Sunday paper as otherwise I'm called a liar and I don't know what I'm talking about. Let the people see the answer in print. I've done business a lot longer than this couple has lived. —Mrs. D.F.

But in the end I couldn't resist her style, so I did her a favor and put it in the Sunday paper. Of course she was right.

Lending institutions record the date they receive the payment, not the date it's mailed. With more and more mortgages being sold to out-of-state banks, many home owners have started paying a few days earlier than they used to, to avoid late charges.

UNFORESEEN PROBLEMS

Dear Edith: Would you kindly tell me of any unforeseen problems that might arise whilst selling a house and holding the mortgage. —Mr. C.K.

Possible problems: The buyers stop paying on the loan. You lent too much and a foreclosure sale will not bring enough to cover the money due. The buyers borrow more money on a second mortgage without telling you. They don't carry fire insurance and when the place burns down, you have nothing left as security but a vacant lot. They don't pay their property taxes, and a tax sale wipes out your claim.

Safeguards: Don't commit yourself unless the buyers furnish a respectable down payment (20 percent is fine) and a satisfactory credit report. Verify their employment and income. Require annual proof that taxes and insurance premiums are paid. Have your own lawyer draw up the mortgage papers to see that they protect you.

I like that "whilst." Are you British?

OUTRAGED AT MORTGAGE DEFAULT

Dear Edith: In 1985 the buyer of my house was short $1,200 at closing, so I took instead a $1,500 mortgage someone owed her on another house. Soon thereafter I began making inquiries directly and through my attorney. The person who owed on the mortgage is now dead and someone else owns that other property; I don't even know who.

My attorney advises against foreclosure because there are probably larger claims against that property and I would lose out completely or incur considerable cost to get a debt-laden house.

I am disappointed that a legally drawn, signed and notarized mortgage purchased in good faith can be ignored by the mortgagor.—Mr. K.N.

And I am disappointed that you saved your inquiries until after you had bought the mortgage. Before lending a total stranger $1,200 (which is what you did) you should have investigated the credit of the borrower, current payment record and the amount already lent against that other house. It wouldn't have hurt to investigate also whether the debtor was alive.

You were probably so elated at the prospect of an extra $300 profit that you didn't stop to suspect you might be paying $1,200 for worthless paper.

There's nothing magic about legally drawn and notarized papers. They are sometimes simply ignored by people (particularly dead ones) who don't pay their bills.

SELLING ON CONTRACT

Dear Edith: I will be 55 soon and because of a painful back injury do not feel I want to continue working. I have no pension program, only meager savings and of course social security at age 62. I do own free and clear a home worth about $120,000 as well as a vacation home.

I am considering selling my home on a contract and living at my lake home. After receiving a sizable down payment, I could collect the balance at 10 percent for 20 years and have approximately $1,000 a month.

Not a lot but I think enough to survive. People I have talked to say to carry the contract is too risky and advise against my plan. —Mr. E.N.F.

Selling on contract, or even selling outright and taking back financing, isn't particularly risky if you screen potential buyers properly. You want that substantial down payment, excellent credit report, and proof of sufficient stable income for them to handle the payments.

Of course, with your plan you'll be in trouble if you live beyond the age of 75. You might want to explore where you'd stand if you received cash for the house and purchased an annuity that would guarantee payments as long as you lived.

BORROWER ISN'T PAYING

Dear Edith: I hold a second mortgage on a duplex I sold in Florida in 1985. Since then the property has been sold twice. The current owner has been consistently one to two months late. It has taken repeated calls and letters each month just to get the payment without the late fee. What can I do? —Mr. N.S.

That borrower owes you not only a late fee, but also extra interest for any month that is skipped. Your legal recourse is to force a sale of the property (foreclose the loan). If the property brought enough at auction to cover the first mortgage and any delinquent property taxes, you'd receive the remaining debt plus (possibly) your legal costs.

Sometimes a lawyer's letter mentioning all this is enough to start prompt payments again. Make it your first step.

LENT TO BROTHER-IN-LAW

Dear Edith: Five years ago we lent my brother-in-law $25,000 because he had a good deal to buy a house. He was supposed to pay us 14 percent interest, which sounded good, and pay the whole thing back in the five years. He pays irregularly and we only have a promissory note.

Now we find out he took out a mortgage on the place, and may have sold half of it to the woman who lives with him. We would like to handle this without making family troubles but are not in a position to throw away money we had planned for our retirement. Can we place a lien on the property, just in case he tries to sell it? If so, how? —Mr. B.T.

Don't worry about making trouble; it isn't you but your brother-in-law who's doing it.

With loans within a family, it is wise to keep things businesslike by using regular mortgage arrangments, which pledge the property as security in case of nonpayment. That's the advice you would have received from a lawyer, if you'd consulted one as you should have before lending on a simple promise to repay.

Take all your papers and records to an attorney now, and ask what you can do. At the least, a lawyer's letter may start payments again.

Your brother-in-law may not realize (and perhaps you don't) that it isn't just a case of being late with his payments. Interest is piling up at a high rate every time he skips a month. He owes you more and more as time goes on.

MORTGAGE AT ONE PERCENT

Dear Edith: Last October at settlement, unexpectedly, I took back a second mortgage when I sold my house. The person wanted it at no interest as they were very strapped for money. The lawyer told me I should charge one percent so I did.

Now I realize that was a mistake and I should have charged more. I'd like to know is there any way I can legally advise them of the error and redo the loan to reflect current rates?—Mrs. E.O.

If you were the borrower, how would you react to a proposal like that?

You must abide by the agreement you signed, and you may be in more trouble than you think. The IRS may tax you as if you had received as much as nine percent. Income tax regulations are complicated when a seller makes a mortgage loan at below-market interest rates.

My lawyer tells me you may have a case against the attorney who got you into this IRS fix; see another lawyer for advice on that point.

SHOULD SHE SELL?

Dear Edith: I am being transferred out of town. I've just been made an offer on my home of $90,000 to $100,000. The prospective buyer wants to assume my existing mortgage of $57,416, take out a second mortgage for $30,000 (if he can get it) and pay me the balance in monthly installments at an interest rate slightly below current lending institutions.

I've never run in to this kind of a proposal before. Is it a wise move on my part, or am I letting myself in for trouble?—Ms. D.W.

Trouble.

How is the buyer going to carry three mortgage payments at once? How good is his credit? What other debts does he have? What is his income? And if it's high enough to make those payments, how come he doesn't have cash for a respectable down payment?

Stay away from this one unless you receive solid-gold answers to those questions.

LENDER DOESN'T SEEM TO WANT MONEY

Dear Edith: I believe I have a very unique problem.

I bought some land about eight years ago and there was a balloon payment on the mortgage due three years ago for about $10,000. After I wrote the seller a couple of registered letters and left messages on his answering machine, he has still not let me know what the exact payoff is. I caught him at his house one day and asked him what the problem was and he said there was none, that he was a procrastinator and he would call me next week. This was over a year ago and I haven't heard from him since.

I would appreciate your advice. I think it's a little ridiculous to have to hire an attorney to pay a man about $10,000. —Mr. H.K.V.

Yep, that's unique all right.

Even if you found out exactly how much is due, you'd be foolish to send a check to a man who must indeed be the world's biggest procrastinator. I wouldn't give much for your chances of receiving in return that vital certificate of satisfaction, acknowleging that the mortgage has been cleared. So you'd better hire a lawyer to handle the payoff.

Did you stop making payments three years ago when the balloon came due? If so, there's a possiblity you owe interest for every month since then—but maybe you don't. Have a lawyer read the mortgage document to figure out where you stand.

Or have you been making payments all along? In that case, of course, you will have reduced the principal further, and you have a sort of holdover mortgage, as if the lender had agreed to extend it. Again, you need a lawyer who can run an amortization schedule and tell you what you owe now.

That's three "see a lawyers" in one answer. I usually try to hold down on them, but it's hard to see what else you can do.

NO PAYMENTS SINCE 1972

Dear Edith: I lent $4,000 to our niece and husband in 1972 to purchase a home. They were supposed to pay monthly with interest. As yet I have had no payments, though I have mentioned it from time to time.

I had a lawyer then to make it all legal and it is registered as a second mortgage. What recourse have we in this case? —Mrs. S.K.

Your niece and her husband are piling up unpaid interest, and at this point probably owe you more than twice the original debt.

Your recourse is to foreclose the loan—force a sale of the property. Whether you'd get your money back would depend on how much the house brought at a public sale, and what other claims were ahead of yours—that first mortgage, possibly back taxes, legal costs of foreclosure.

You probably wouldn't want to force your niece's family out anyhow, but perhaps a lawyer's letter mentioning the possibility—and the increasing debt—would get things moving.

CHAPTER 16

Assumed Mortgages

"Would we have the right to reclaim the property?"

In areas of the country where house prices have gone up steadily, no one worries much about liability for an old mortgage that was assumed by the next owner of the property. But in recent years, sellers in farm states or oil-dependent states have seen values drop, and they're the ones who write to the newspaper for information on assumptions. No funny letters in this batch.

CAUGHT ON FHA ASSUMPTION

Dear Edith: The couple who bought my house three years ago by assuming my FHA mortgage left town, were unable to sell the house, simply walked out.

I contacted an attorney who claimed the lender could secure a default judgment against me for any deficit resulting from the foreclosed sale price. If the loan is secured by the FHA, why should I be liable to the bank?—Ms. F.B.

Because that's the way it is. Yes, the FHA will reimburse the lender for any shortfall, but after that they'll come looking for you.

The mortgage you signed pledged the real estate as security for the debt. That gave the lender the right to sell the property.

Your problem comes with the other paper you signed—the note, or bond. That was a personal promise to repay the money, and letting the next owners assume the mortgage didn't release you from that promise.

ASSUMING VA AND FHA

Dear Edith: I heard that FHA and VA came out with a new ruling or law that when anyone assumes either type of loan they must qualify as if getting a new loan.

What I would like to know is when is the cutoff date for being able to assume an existing FHA or VA loan without having to qualify.—Mr. E.D.

For all VA loans placed after March 1, 1988, the person who assumes the mortgage must prove qualification to the lending institution. Older VA mortgages can still be taken over by the next owner without bank approval. In either case, the new owner need not be a veteran.

Cutoff date for FHA loans is December 1, 1986. Any FHA mortgage loan made before that date is assumable with no credit check. With FHA loans made between that date and early 1990, free assumability depends on the age of the loan.

Newer FHA loans are assumable only by buyers who prove financial ability to pay. There is, of course, substantial saving on closing costs, for although a credit check and other verification are required, no new appraisal of the property is required, neither is title insurance nor (in those states that have it) mortgage tax. The loan remains at its original interest rate.

ASSUMING A VA LOAN

Dear Edith: We are putting our house up for sale and my husband has a VA mortgage on it. Can we let anyone at all take it over?—Mrs. P.I.

Yes, if you originally took out the loan before March 1, 1988.

GETTING THE HOUSE BACK

Dear Edith: When I sold my condo, I let someone assume my FHA loan on it. I sought advice from experts, including my agent and my lending institution, as to the extent of my liability under an assumption. I was told that if the new owners defaulted, and I became liable for the loan, I would have no problem. I would get the property back and be able to resell it. I could not find any literature on the subject with information to the contrary.

Now I find out that I would not get the property back, nor would I have any control over its resale. Which is correct?—T.L.

Many people think "you'd get the property back" but that's not the way it works.

If the buyer of your house defaults on your old FHA loan, the property will be seized and sold, but not by you. If an auction sale brings enough to cover unpaid property taxes, legal costs and the remaining FHA debt, you're okay. If it doesn't bring enough to clear the mortgage, you could be responsible for the shortfall.

FROM THE BUYER'S VIEWPOINT

Dear Edith: What should I look for in a desirable assumption?—Mr. L.N.

Some mortgages ("freely assumable") can be taken over by any later owner of the property. Others ("assumable with lender's approval") can be assumed by anyone who proves financial qualifications. Still others cannot be assumed at all and must be paid off when the property is sold.

When assuming a mortgage you will be concerned, of course, with present interest rate and whether the lender has the right to change the rate at an assumption. If it's an adjustable rate loan, you need a complete explanation of how and when the rate can be changed.

You want to know whether that particular loan requires you to prove financial qualification to the lender (some do, some don't) and whether you'll owe any points or assumption fee.

Beyond that, you want proof that the mortgage has been paid up-to-date, and a statement from the lender certifying how much is still owed, how long the mortgage has to run, and the exact amount of monthly payments.

NEW OWNER NOT INTERESTED

Dear Edith: How would a person go about getting their name off a mortgage when the title is signed over to someone else who is not too interested in the responsibility of assuming it? Can the title holder be forced to assume the mortgage?—Ms. H.F.

The time to make sure a new owner takes responsibility for an assumed mortgage is when signing the agreement for sale or transfer of title. I know of no way to force it afterwards.

Some complicated paperwork might enable the new borrower to take full responsibility and let the previous owner off completely. That procedure, however, requires full cooperation from the new owner, which sounds as if it's lacking here.

MESS WITH THE VA

Dear Edith: Two years ago we decided to sell our home. It was suggested we let someone assume our VA mortgage. We asked the broker what would happen if the person defaulted and were told it would not hurt our credit. The broker found an acquaintance to assume our loan.

Our old mortgage company recently called to tell us payments on the house were six months behind. We found the buyers had moved out taking the appliances and leaving the place in a shambles. It looks as if there will be a loss *of about $15,000, counting repairs. The VA tells us we are responsible. Can they take our savings? We have had excellent credit until this time. We feel we were naive for getting into this situation but are angry at the broker and the buyer for their part. —N.R.T.*

There's no practical use in being angry at the buyer; you can't get blood out of a stone, especially one that's moved away.

But the broker is another matter, and it's worth talking with a lawyer at this point. As I see it, the broker advised you to allow an assumption by a buyer who was financially unsound, and misinformed you about your liability. Perhaps the broker also wrongly advised that you didn't need a lawyer back there. Surely an attorney would have informed you of your liability and helped you check out the buyers.

It will help if you can prove the broker misled you. In any case you need an attorney's help to get through this, as well as advice on whether you can expect the agent to bear some or all of your loss.

WHO GETS THE REFUND?

Dear Edith: In a recent column you stated that where a refund of unused FHA mortgage premium is due, it goes to the person making the last payment. I've been told that it depends on whether the mortgage assumption was formal or informal. If it was informal, the refund goes to the person who was still responsible for the mortgage (usually the initial home owner.) True or false? —Mr. H.T.

There is, of course, a difference between a formal assumption of an FHA loan, with the next borrower proving qualification to the lender; and an informal one, where the buyer just takes over the house and the mortgage, and the original borrower retains liability.

I just called the FHA refund office in Washington, and you might want to try them—202/755-5616. After you get the line, press "0" to talk with a real person.

The answer I got was that the refund, if any, does go to the person paying off the loan, and that it wouldn't make any difference if the assumption were a formal one or not.

If you try it and get a different answer, or if you can tell me where you got the contradictory information, I'd appreciate hearing from you again.

VETERAN STILL LIABLE

Dear Edith: Three years ago I was divorced. As it ended up my ex-wife paid me $4,000 and I signed over the house on a quit-claim deed. The loan was *under both our names with my VA entitlement. If she defaults on the loan what happens?—Mr. W.H.*

You signed a promise to repay that loan, and you are still liable.

EX-HUSBAND ON THE MORTGAGE

Dear Edith: My husband and I were recently divorced. He signed over the house to me on a quit-claim deed. However, his name is still on the mortgage. He now wants to buy another piece of property and wants his name off the mortgage. Can't it be done now that a quit-claim deed has been filed? Is there any way to get his name off the mortgage except refinancing?—E.L.

If your own financial situation is strong enough, perhaps you can go through some paperwork to relieve him of liability. Your lawyer, or your ex-husband's lawyer, can look into the matter.

CHAPTER 17

Selling and the IRS

"...because Uncle Sam says so, that's why."

I didn't set out to write a tax column, and I'm not an accountant—but so many questions come in on the tax consequences of selling a home that I've developed some expertise in the subject.

Often, by the time people write to the column, they've already heard the bad news about their income tax liability—but hope springs eternal and they're hoping I'll tell them something different. There are some ingenious taxpayers out there, witness the following letter.

DEDUCTING INTEREST AGAIN

Dear Edith: When we sell our home, may we deduct as an expense the interest we've paid to our bank over the past 13 years?—N.H.

Interest paid on your mortgage was deductible every year; you can't deduct it again. Sorry.

EX-HUSBAND'S LIABILITY

Dear Edith: I quit-claimed half my home to my husband ten years ago in return for his taking care of me and my children. We later divorced and sold the house. He gets half due to my stupidity but doesn't he have some taxation somewhere along the line? He had only $1,000 when we got married and now he is a lot richer with no investment!—Ms. R.V.

I don't understand why you're worrying about your ex-husband's tax liability. At any rate, he hasn't asked me, so it's none of my business.

TAX BREAK ON SECOND HOME

Dear Edith: Last year, I rented my second home for eight months. I had the house vacant since then. When I filed the tax return, I claimed it as rental property, claimed depreciation etc. Now I want to sell this house.

Is it legal to consider it as a second home sale? If it is, how long can I keep the money before I have to use it to buy another second home? —V.O.

There's no special tax break on profit from the sale of sale of a second home, whether it's been rented out or not. Sorry about that.

TAX ON INHERITED COTTAGE

Dear Edith: We inherited a summer cottage seven years ago and recently sold it. We were told we'd have to pay tax on the whole selling price since we paid nothing for it. Now in your column I read my capital gain would be the difference between value now and value seven years ago. If so, who determines these values? —G.O.

Today's value is easy—it's your sale price.

As for cost basis: When you inherited the place seven years ago, it was probably appraised as part of estate settlement. The lawyer who handled the estate may have the figure. Otherwise, ask a real estate broker active in that area for a written estimate of value as of the date of death.

SELLING FATHER'S CROPLAND

Dear Edith: I own 60 acres of cropland. My father acquired this land for a very small sum in 1933. He deeded it to me in 1949 but it was not recorded until 1956, when I began paying the taxes. My accountant once told me that this was a gift from my father so the cost basis would go back to his original cost in 1933, leaving me with a large capital gain tax, should I wish to sell. Thank you for any ideas. —Mr. S.G.

No ideas—your accountant was right. Because you received the land as a gift, your cost basis is the same as your father's would have been— "cost in the hands of the donor."

SELLING HIS MOTHER'S HOME

Dear Edith: In 1981 my mother "sold" her home to me for $1. A gift tax return was filed and a figure of $20,000 was reached as her cost basis. The market value of the home then was $35,000.

Next month I will be moving my mother to a retirement home and selling her home to my cousin for $52,000. It is my understanding that the proceeds of this sale will have to be included as regular income on my tax return. I am hoping you will shed some light on possible tax breaks that will benefit me. —Mr. W.A.

No special tax breaks if the place is not your own residence.

Because you received the house as a gift, your profit will be figured from your mother's cost basis—$20,000, not, I am afraid, the $35,000 figure. You can add to that basis any money spent over the years for permanent improvements. Your taxable profit will be $52,000 minus that cost basis and a few other expenses of selling.

BECAUSE UNCLE SAM SAYS SO

Dear Edith: We gave our son a rental house for graduation. We were told that when he sells it he will be taxed on the difference between what we paid for it ten years ago and the present value. Why does this differ from inherited assets that use the value at the time of death as the cost?

Also, we are 45 years old and have a large home. We would like to live in a simpler less expensive one. Must we continue here for another ten years in order not to lose the equity we have gained by paying income tax on the difference? There seems no way out. —K.T.

Yes, your son takes over your old cost basis on the rental house. Yes, he could have had a stepped-up basis if he hadn't received it until your death. Yes, you can't take that $125,000 tax-free profit until you're 55.

Why? Just because Uncle Sam says so.

INHERITING FROM DAUGHTER

Dear Edith: I read in a column you wrote about tax laws sheltering gains on inherited property. But how are capital gains treated when your daughter dies and wills her home to her father and mother? This is the reverse case of the one in your column. —Mr. O.K.E.

Same ruling. No difference whether the asset is inherited from one's parent, a child or a stranger. The heir takes it with a stepped-up cost basis, current value at time of death.

TAX ON GIFT PROPERTY

Dear Edith: I read your article saying there would be no taxable profit on inherited property. Our mother gave my brother and I a quit claim deed to her home. She passed away 2-1/2 years ago and we sold the house this year. The real estate broker said we would receive a 1099 form. Do I have to pay income tax and if so what forms would we have to fill out?—Mr. N.V.S.

First off, you didn't inherit that house, you received it as a gift. From an income tax point of view, there's a big difference. Because you got it as a gift, profit is figured from your mother's original cost for the house, plus any permanent improvements over the years.

The fact that you receive a form 1099 isn't as important as the fact that a copy goes to the IRS, letting them know you sold the property. Your income tax returns had better match up. You report the sale on schedule D; you may want professional help with your return for the year in which you sell a house.

As for inherited property—I said there probably would be little or no taxable profit if it were sold soon after, not two-and-a-half years after, the original owner died.

MOTHER HAS NO WILL

Dear Edith: My mother is a widow and very seriously ill. She does not have a will, but she expressed her desire to leave her home to me and her granddaughter. The house is paid off and worth approximately $250,000 to $300,000. She has no other assets.

She would like us to sell the house when she dies. Can she write her own will now? If she paid $27,000 for the house, how much will we be taxed? How to handle this situation?—Mrs. K.N.

Your mother must write a will immediately. Otherwise the state will decide who gets her property, and it may not be what she—or you—would expect.

If she writes it herself, the will may or may not be legally valid. Have a lawyer do it properly. The matter is important.

If your mother gives you the house before she dies, when it is sold income tax would be due on at least $223,000 profit (capital gain). If she leaves it in a will, there will be little or no income tax due after the sale. And if she leaves less than $600,000, no federal estate tax will be due.

THE ULTIMATE TAX SHELTER

Dear Edith: Suddenly I realized I had a problem and I respectfully solicit your view. My wife and I are both 74 and if we sold our home today might realize a $50,000 tax-exempt gain. So far no problem.

But were my wife and I to die suddenly, together, how would the Internal Revenue Service treat the capital gain when our heirs inherit the property?

Our will carefully identifies our son and daughter to jointly receive and dispose of our property. —Mr. S.C.

No problem. Death is the ultimate tax shelter.

Your cost basis would be forgotten; your kids would inherit your home at current value. If they sold soon thereafter, they'd have little or no taxable profit. And unless your estate ran higher than $600,000, they'd have no federal estate tax either.

WRONG 1099 SENT

Dear Edith: My mother gave her home to my brother and me, and after her death this February we sold it for $90,000 and divided the money.

Our problem: a form 1099 was sent to IRS in each our names for the amount of $90,000. How do we show the IRS we only each received one-half that amount? —T.O.V.

It's a simple matter for the person or institution that handled the closing to file corrected form 1099s with the IRS, showing that you and your brother each sold only $45,000 worth of house. Insist that they do so before the end of the year.

Follow up; the matter is important. If you don't get proof that the correction was filed, mention that you'll hold the closer responsible for any tax foul-up, penalties, legal or accounting fees you might run into.

IRS REPORT SEEMS WRONG

Dear Edith: I represented my sister at the sale of her house since she was out of town. Now she has received a copy of a 1099 report to the IRS, showing that she received full payment for the house. She only received $10,000 down payment, and will get the rest over the next 15 years. Shouldn't the form show the down payment rather than the full purchase price?

Will this make trouble for her? I feel partly responsible for the closing. What forms do we need to file for the correction? —Ms. S.S.

Nothing to worry about.

The 1099 form sent to the IRS properly shows full sale price. Then your sister—or better, her accountant—lists the details in her income tax return next April, to determine her current tax liability.

CONVERTING BACK TO OWN HOME

Dear Edith: I know the tax laws regarding the deferment of capital gains on one's primary residence and the one-time exclusion for people over 55, but I have been unable to get a satisfactory answer to my situation.

My primary residence was converted to rental property in 1984. Now I would like to return to the house and then put it up for sale. The IRS does not specify a time period for occupancy before I can defer the gain, only that it must be my primary residence. Can you help?—Mr. D.N.

If you intend to use that one-time over-55 $125,000 exclusion, the matter is clear. You must own the property and occupy it as your main residence for three of the five years before you sell. If you moved back today, you'd have to occupy it for the next three years to qualify.

If you're asking about the other home-seller's tax break, the chance to postpone tax if you buy a more expensive replacement home within two years of selling the first one, the answer is not so simple. Changing the house back to your own main residence is possible, and I suspect one year's occupancy before the sale may be enough. But check it out with your own tax lawyer or CPA.

Whether or not you eventually owe tax on your profit, the calculation of that profit will take into account the depreciation you have claimed over the years.

GIFTS TO GRANDCHILDREN

Dear Edith: When my father died his property was left to my two brothers and myself. Now my brothers are deceased and the property is solely mine. When I sell, I understand capital gains tax would have to be paid on the difference between the sale price and the amount it was appraised for when my last brother died.

Since this is family property I would like to give a token sum to each of my father's grandchildren. Am I required to pay the full capital gains tax first? Would these grandchildren be subject to a gift tax on the amount they receive? —Mr. D.P.

Your cost basis for that property is more complex than you would believe—possibly a different cost for each one-third you own, then all three added together. If you are the sole owner, you pay the tax on profit.

You may give up to $10,000 a year each of those grandchildren ($20,000 each if you're married or they're married) with no federal gift tax due from you or them.

PROPERTY FOR SERVICES

Dear Edith: For services rendered (mowing, brush-cutting, painting and general upkeep) I received a deed in 1983 to two acres of land. No money changed hands.

Since then the property has greatly increased in value. What would my tax liability be if I were to sell now?—Mr. B.N.

When you receive a gift, your cost basis is the value of the property "in the hands of the donor"—in other words, whatever the cost basis was to the person who gave it to you.

If you received the place in return for services, that complicates matters (your income tax liability for 1983, for example.) Maybe you'll want to regard it as a simple gift after all.

NO RECEIPTS OR BILLS

Dear Edith: When I sell my house, I am aware that I can add to the original cost the improvements, windows, driveway, garage etc. I have not kept a record of these expenses or bills. How do I substantiate these costs to the IRS to bring up the real cost of my house?—Mr. V.C.

Estimate the cost of improvements as best you can. If your tax return were ever questioned, you'd be asked to substantiate the figures, but you are entitled to claim those improvements as part of your cost basis.

Every home owner should keep a separate file or house book, with cancelled checks and bills for permanent improvements (as opposed to repairs).

DECEMBER OR JANUARY?

Dear Edith: Should I sell a piece of undeveloped land in December or January? The contract says whichever I wish, and it's for cash. Most of it will be a capital gain.—Ms. M.V.

If you sell in December, you receive your money one month earlier. But you wait until January, you postpone paying income tax on your profit for a whole year. One way you'd pay the tax in April; the other way in the following April. This gives you the full use of your money for an extra 12 months.

Consult an accountant, however, to see if your particular situation would call for quarterly estimated tax payments along the way.

VERY IMPORTANT QUESTION

Dear Edith: Could you please answer a question for me? It is very important to me.

If a husband and wife own a home but do not get along any longer will they lose all of the profits from the home if they sell before the age of 55? They both have worked very hard. This is very important as the profits would make a new life for them both. P.S. The home is in both names.—M.T.

If a home is sold before either of the owners is 55, the $125,000 exclusion isn't available. But the chance to roll over profit for postponed tax does exist, even if the home is replaced by two different ones when they separate. Either seller may postpone tax on his or her share of profit by buying a replacement home within two years. If they shared the proceeds equally, the replacement home would have to cost half of what the old one sold for to take full advantage of that tax break.

Otherwise the profit will be subject to income tax. That won't, of course, take all the money. Think of profit like extra salary—you'd pay tax on it, but you'd still get to keep some.

TAX-DEFERRED EXCHANGE

Dear Edith: We are considering selling our four-apartment rental building with a view to purchasing a similar building in another area. How can we plan for tax-deferred status?—S. and U.C.

By talking everything over in advance with a real estate lawyer who is familiar with the process. Tax-deferred exchanges require careful planning and timing.

TAX BREAK FOR DISABLED

Dear Edith: When you sell a house, is there any federal tax break on capital gain for the disabled?—S.G.

No.

NEGATIVE AMORTIZATION AND IRS

Dear Edith: Four years ago we took out a negative amortization loan on our house. The interest rate was 15.5 percent. We started making payments at 10.5 percent with the additional interest we didn't pay being added to our original loan amount. By now we've added an additional $10,000 to what we owe.

When we sell the house and pay off the loan, can we claim that $10,000 as an income tax deduction for interest?—Mrs. S.G.

The IRS tells me that your payoff statement from the bank should include a clear designation of that extra $10,000 as postponed interest. If it does, you can claim it as a deduction.

SOLD HOME AT A LOSS

Dear Edith: I sold my own home last year and had a loss of about $10,000. I'm told I can't deduct the loss. Do I report it anywhere on my income tax return?—Mr. W.K.

Yes, even though you have no income tax consequences, you must mention the sale on your return. All sales of single- to four-family houses are reported to the IRS. You'll want your return to match up with the information Uncle Sam already has.

You report it on IRS form 2119, Sale or Exchange of Principal Residence.

CHAPTER 18

Postponing Tax on Profit

"Is there a tax break if I reinvest in savings bonds?"

There are two delightful special federal income tax breaks for sellers: the senior citizens' one-time exclusion from tax of up to $125,000 profit (to be discussed in the next chapter) and the opportunity—in fact the requirement—for federal income tax on profit to be postponed when a taxpayer of any age replaces a principal residence with another of equal or greater value within two years. Plenty of complications. What if the next home costs less? If you sell at a loss? If your home also includes a store or office?

WITHIN TWO-YEAR PERIOD

Dear Edith: We will be retiring in two years. We do not want to sell our home yet. If we buy a new home before we sell the old one, will we lose the chance to postpone tax on our profit? (We prefer not to take the "once in a lifetime" at this time.) —E.E.

Home owners of any age may postpone income tax on all of their profit if a replacement residence of equal or greater value is bought within two years of the sale of their present main home. This provision would apply if you bought the next home two years before or two years after selling your present one.

NEXT HOME COST LESS

Dear Edith: What if you buy another home for less than you sold your first one for? Sold home for $150,000. Bought another within two years for $100,000. Do I owe the government? —S.N.

Up to $50,000 in profit (if you had that much) is immediately taxable. Sorry about that—but any further profit will not be taxable until you sell the next home.

REPLACING SUMMER COTTAGE

Dear Edith: We are selling our summer cottage at a large profit. How long do we have before we buy a ski-area condo instead, to postpone income tax? —Mr. D.S.

Take all the time you want, because there isn't any federal income tax break on the sale of a second home. Your profit will be immediately taxable.

REMODELING THE HOUSE

Dear Edith: We will be selling our home and moving into a rental property we've owned for five years. We plan to rebuild the rental home, add a second story etc. Will this let us postpone tax on the profit from our present home? Does it count toward "must buy another residence of equal or greater value" to roll over capital gains from sale of current residence?—T.G.C.

Anything you spend in permanent improvements on your next home within two years counts as if you were spending it to buy that replacement residence. Your outlay for rebuilding may not be as much as you receive for your present home, but you should be able to shield at least part of your profit from immediate income tax.

OFF TO LONDON

Dear Edith: We may be transferred to London soon. We would sell our home and would like to postpone payment of capital gains tax. In a few years we could be back here buying another home. I know the time limit for buying a replacement residence is two years. Does that apply if we are living out of the country?—Mrs. T.W.

IRS publication #523, "Tax Information on Selling Your Home," is free for the asking. Call 1/800-424-1040 and ask for a copy to be sent to you.

The pamphlet says the two-year replacement period can be extended as much as another two years while you have your tax home (place where you live and work) outside the United States.

MAKING HOME IMPROVEMENTS

Dear Edith: I intend to sell my current home and purchase another immediately. The new house will cost $50K less than my current home, but I will immediately put about $75K into new home improvements. Does this improvement money result in a "more expensive home" for tax postponement?—Mr. D.E.

Yes, it does. The Internal Revenue Service says the purchase price of your replacement home includes buying or building, rebuilding, and capital improvements or additions. You can include any costs incurred within two years before or after you sell the present home.

TAX RETURN ON SELLING

Dear Edith: We just sold our home and purchased a more expensive one. When do we compute the capital gain, or isn't it necessary since the new house cost more than the selling price of the first house? We are both 50 years old and will be entitled to the capital gains exclusion in five years.—Mr. K.O.T.

Yes, you must compute your gain. No, you won't owe tax on it at this time. Yes, you must list the sale on this year's income tax return, on form 2119.

LIVING IN HALF THE HOUSE

Dear Edith: We have owned this two-family house and lived in one side for 12 years. Now we are going to sell it and buy a small ranch. We expect to sell for about $200,000, which represents $80,000 profit. Must we buy a replacement home for $200,000 or more, in order to postpone tax on our profit? —Mrs. L.R.

The IRS will consider that you have two sales here.

The first one is the sale of income property (the other side of the house) for $100,000. Profit on that side will be $40,000 and it will be taxable. (Actually, your profit will probably be greater, because you may have overlooked the need to reduce your cost basis by the depreciation you've been claiming every year on your tax return.)

Your second transaction is the sale of your own residence, for $100,000. If you buy a replacement home within two years costing $100,000 or more, tax on that half of your profit will be postponed.

WAS THE IRS WRONG?

Dear Edith: I am selling my home and have already used my one-time exclusion. The Internal Revenue Service has told me the following on the phone: If my house cost $120,000 and I sold it for $200,000, I would have a $80,000 gain. If I bought another house and invested the $80,000 gain, I would defer the tax until the sale of that next home. I would like to have that verified. I heard a man on the radio state the whole $200,000 would have to be reinvested to postpone tax. I hope the IRS has given me correct information but sometimes they are wrong.—B.C.

And this time they were—or you heard wrong. In order to postpone tax on your whole profit, you must buy a replacement residence costing at least as much as the old one sells for, $200,000. You need not reinvest the exact dollars you receive; it's the two sale prices that count.

INVESTING INHERITED MONEY

Dear Edith: If money is inherited, then invested in real estate immediately, how will this affect how much tax you must pay on the money?—F.G., Sr.

No effect at all.

SELLING THE A-FRAME

Dear Edith: As part of a divorce settlement, I received five acres of land with an A-frame cottage. We paid $1,000 for the land in 1970 and built the cottage ourselves. I should get about $65,000 for it.

Would it be possible to avoid the capital gains tax if I use the money to pay off the mortgage on my home?—S.E.

No, it wouldn't.

INVESTING IN TAX-FREE SAVINGS

Dear Edith: I understand that if you sell a home and buy another home within two years you can postpone income tax on your profit. If, instead of buying a new home you invest in a tax-free savings plan for your child's education, do you still have to pay tax on the profit from the sale of your home?—W.S.

Yes, you do. Savings bonds do not count as a replacement residence. Sorry.

BUILDING IT HIMSELF

Dear Edith: We are selling our present home and moving to another we will build. After purchasing a piece of land, installing the septic system and well, my husband will build our new house himself. After taking the total cost of land and building materials, what happens if it does not exceed the sale price of our first residence? Will we be taxed? How is my husband's labor accounted for in building the new home?—E.W.

It doesn't count.

The IRS will consider only your actual expenses. If this totals less than the sale price of your present house, then part of your profit will be immediately taxable. Part may qualify for postponed taxes.

If you are building, remember that you have a deadline. You must occupy the replacement residence within two years of selling the first home, in order to use the tax break at all.

GOOD NEWS AND BAD NEWS

Dear Edith: Two questions:

1. *If one sells a principal residence and buys two houses, one to be used as a principal residence and the other to be a rental property, can the cost of both houses be used to defer the payment of tax on profit from the first house?*
2. *If one sells a principal residence and buys a fixer-upper, can you include the money to fix up the second house as part of its cost in order to defer income taxes on profit from the original house?*

The first seems unlikely, but the second seems likely.—B.N.

And you're right both times. First question, no. Second question, yes, if the second house is one's own residence and the improvements are made within 24 months of the first sale.

OFFICE IN HOME

Dear Edith: For 10 years I have maintained an office in my home. My wife and I would like to move to a more expensive home. Does the depreciation I have claimed on my income taxes for this office have to be paid back when we buy another house? If depreciation repayment is necessary can I avoid it by not claiming a home office for a year?—L.C.

The depreciation you have claimed (or could have claimed) reduces your cost basis for the house, from which profit is computed. Most of your profit qualifies for postponed tax treatment, rolled over into the cost basis of your next home. Whatever percentage of the house you have claimed for office use, that percentage of your profit would be immediately taxable.

Yes, it may be possible to return the whole house to use as a primary residence before you sell. Discuss that one with your accountant.

CHAPTER 19

That $125,000 Tax Break

"Why couldn't this couple get a cheapie divorce, then..."

What one topic brings more mail to the column every year? No contest—hands down—it's that $125,000 exclusion. Everyone loves thinking about it, planning for it, and it's almost the only free lunch offered by the IRS. But the complications are endless. The most common problem comes when one marries someone who has already used that once-in-a-lifetime exclusion, and my answer is always disappointing. Sometimes I'm tempted to suggest the older couple just live in sin till the next sale is completed.

I've received thousands of questions on this topic and each one is slightly different. This first one, though, is the most different one yet.

COMMISSION AND $125,000

Dear Edith: About that $125,000 income tax break, I would like to know when I sell my house does a broker charge commission on the full sale price or after the $125,000 is deducted?—Mr. K.V.

The $125,000 figure applies to your income tax return, and has nothing to do with your arrangements with a real estate broker.

WHAT MAKES A SALE?

Dear Edith: We have a retirement home and would like to move into it as soon as possible after age 55, to take advantage of the tax exclusion of profit on our present home. So we don't make any mistake, we would like to know what constitutes a sale, accepting the offer, or the closing date. This would give us a guide when to put the house up for sale.—Mrs. S.K.

You can accept an offer ahead of time, but don't actually transfer title until your 55th birthday.

NINE MONTHS A YEAR

Dear Edith: I am the owner of seasonal property where I live for eight or nine months a year. Is it possible for me to receive the $125,000 tax exclusion on this property should I decide to sell it?—Mrs. F.D.

The IRS says your principal residence is the place where you spend most of your time. Eight or nine months a year should qualify you for special home-seller's tax treatment.

LAST THREE YEARS ENOUGH

Dear Edith: I hope you can answer this as I seem to be getting all different answers from people who are supposed to be in the know. It pertains to the exclusion of gain ($125,000) on the sale of a home. I understand over 55 years and only used once. What I don't understand is the so-called three of five years.

I bought my home in June 1989. If I kept it as my main residence until June 1992, could I claim exclusion or would I have to wait to sell till June 1994?—Mr. K.N.

You must own and occupy your home three of the five years before the sale to claim the exclusion. If they are only the three years just before the sale, that's enough. You're eligible if the house were sold any time after June 1992.

PAYING OFF LOAN

Dear Edith: My husband just turned 55 and we would like to sell our home. We have an FHA improvement loan, through a credit union. Is it permissible to pay off the loan with the proceeds of the sale? Can we get the over-55 income tax exemption if we do?—Mrs. T.W.

You can certainly use sale proceeds to pay off loans on your property. It's a common practice. Doing so has no effect on income tax treatment.

You can choose to take this particular tax break whether you buy another home or move to an apartment, and the IRS pays no attention to the mortgage situation on the property.

RENTING BEFORE THE SALE

Dear Edith: I have called IRS four different times and received four different answers so I hope you can help me. I am 64 years old, own my home and lived in it for six years. Then I rented it out and moved to an apartment where I pay rent. I've been out of my home for 17 months.

The question is if I sell my house this year would I be entitled to the $125,000 tax exclusion?—Mrs. N.B.

I once took a similar question to IRS research, and a month later received a detailed phone call with what was described as a definitive answer.

At your age, and assuming you never used this one-time tax break before: You can take up to $125,000 profit free of federal income tax, as long as you owned and occupied the house yourself for at least three of the five years before the sale. The fact that you rented the house out for part of the time doesn't matter. For this particular tax break only, it doesn't even matter if the place is no longer your principal residence by the time you sell.

Be sure to arrange the sale so that settlement takes place before you've been out for two years.

LIVES IN ONE APARTMENT

Dear Edith: I own a four-unit apartment building which I have lived in for the past 26 years. During this time I have become widowed but plan to work until I am 65.

I live in one apartment and rent the other three units out. During the years I have declared the income of course and have offset it by three-fourths of the allowable expenses.

When I retire I may sell the building. May I consider this as my principal residence and take the one-time $125,000 untaxed profit allowance since I have lived nowhere else?—B.Y.U.

The Internal Revenue Service will look upon your sale as two separate transactions, one the sale of your own home, the other the sale of income property.

You can use the home-owner's tax exclusion to cover one-quarter of your profit. The remaining three-quarters will be subject to income tax.

TWO-OWNER TAX BREAK

Dear Edith: My friend and I bought an unusual two-family house in 1980. He lives upstairs, I live downstairs. We are both senior citizens. If we were to sell our house now we could get at least $350,000. Would we each get the $125,000 exclusion being that we are each an owner, or is it allowed to only one owner? We have never used the exclusion before.—Mrs. N.O'B.

The IRS states clearly that if two persons not married to each other own and occupy the place as a main residence, each may take a full $125,000 exclusion on his or her share of profit. A brother and sister, for example, or you and your friend, could have a total of up to $250,000 profit on the sale of a long-time home, free of any federal income tax ever.

USED THE EXCLUSION BEFORE

Dear Edith: My husband and I sold our principal residence in 1966. I was 53, he was 66 years old. On the strength of his age, we took the one-time tax exclusion.

He has since died. If I sell my principal residence now can I take the exclusion, since I am alone and over the age of 65?—Mrs. L.F.

The current age requirement for the one-time tax break is 55, not 65. And if your husband had used this exclusion, you could not take it now—but, here's the good news—he didn't.

It looks as if your husband used a different tax break in 1966. The current $125,000 exclusion went into effect on July 26, 1978, and you are entitled to one crack at this one.

WIDOW AND WIDOWER MARRYING

Dear Edith: I am a 68-year-old widow and am engaged to a 77-year-old widower. I am going to sell my home before we get married, so I can get my $125,000 tax-free profit. If we get married and I go to live in his home for a year or so and then he sells, will he be able to get his $125,000 tax-free profit? Or does he have to sell his home also before we get married, to qualify for it himself?—I.S.

If he's married when he sells his home, and his spouse has previously used the exclusion, he's out of luck. He'd have to sell before you married, in order to use the exclusion himself.

Best wishes for your happiness.

HUSBAND DID USE IT

Dear Edith: I'm asking for information regarding the selling of my house and taking advantage of the one-time, over 55, $125,000 exclusion of profit from income tax.

I'm 57, remarried and in my own home and have never used the exclusion. My husband is 72 and his wife (now dead) used the exclusion before. The home they sold then was in her name only.—Mrs. C.D.

I'll bet you already know the answer, and just wrote hoping I'd say it isn't so. That exclusion only works if neither spouse has ever used it before. Your husband used it when he signed his tax return the year his wife sold the home that was in her name. You're out of luck.

WIDOW AND WIDOWER MARRIED

Dear Edith: I have a house but my husband died. I married a man that has a house but his spouse died. For each of us our house is our sole asset (all else went for spouses' medical bills).

Will we be penalized if we sell one or should we rent it or what? We are both putting children through college. We would appreciate any information about this predicament. — Mr. and Mrs. K.E.

I'm not sure what you mean by being penalized on a sale. Unless one of you ever did it before, you and your husband are entitled to sell one long-time home (if the owner is at least 55 and hasn't been out of the home more than two years) free from any federal income tax on profit up to $125,000. You couldn't do that with both your houses, but you can with one.

As for keeping the extra house and renting it out, find out how much rent you could expect to receive. Estimate what you'd have left after expenses — property tax, insurance, upkeep, occasional vacancies. Then compare that with the income you'd have if you sold the house and put the proceeds into long-term savings. To make a better decision, talk with an accountant about the difference in after-tax income.

If you kept the house and it went up in value, you'd continue to build equity. You'd owe income tax on your profit when you eventually sold, but you'd still have that one-shot home-owner's tax break to use some day on the other house, the one you will be living in.

The drawback is that it takes a certain temperament to be a landlord. A rented house doesn't just sit there like a CD drawing interest. It needs attention, and can bring headaches if you don't act carefully.

HUSBAND LEFT NO WILL

Dear Edith: When my husband died, he didn't leave a will. I had to go to court. The property was divided so my daughter, my son and I each own one-third of the house I live in. Now I'm ready to retire. If I sell this property would I get the tax break of $125,000 tax-free profit? — Mrs. N.W.

It would probably apply only to your one-third of the profit; your son's and daughter's shares would be fully taxable. Your letter illustrates once more how foolish it is to put off making a will. When the state determines how property is divided, things may not go the way one would have wished.

PERMANENT RESIDENT OF FLORIDA

Dear Edith: Please explain what is a primary home. I own a home up North that I have lived in for 16 years. I also own a condo in Florida. I would like to sell my old home and get the special tax break. I am now an official resident of Florida. Does that make a difference?—Mr. J.M.

I've heard from many people who've gone to great trouble establishing themselves as Florida residents—voting, driver's license, tax returns etc. Then they wonder if they can use the special home-sellers' tax treatment on their long-time year-round homes.

    The IRS booklet on the subject, publication #523, states clearly that if you have two homes, your primary residence is the one where you spend more of your time. I called the IRS and was told they stand by that test. They said that except in rare borderline situations, that's their standard for judging.

MUST SHE SELL?

Dear Edith: I live in a senior citizen housing complex, where I rent. I had to move in when my name came up, earlier than I had expected. Recently I read that if you rent public housing you must sell your home within two years.

    My son lives in my house as caretaker and we are fixing it for resale. Is it true that the property must be sold within the two year time limit?—L.B.

As far as I know, you could keep your house forever, leave it to your son, give it away, whatever you wanted. I know of no requirement that you sell within two years, unless your particular senior complex has such a rule.

    If you intended to use that senior citizen's one-time income tax break on profit, you would indeed have to sell within two years.

HOW BIG A HALF?

Dear Edith: We live in one side of our duplex and rent the other. Both of us are over 55 and eligible for the one-time home-seller's tax break. I am aware that I must pay income tax on the sale of the rental side of the house if we sell.

    But do we have to pay tax on exactly half the selling price? Or can we have an appraisal done and pay tax on the percentage the appraiser thinks the rental side is worth? Our side is 80 square feet larger, has had considerable remodeling and has an extra room in the basement.—Mrs. O.R.

When you put a new roof on the house, what percentage did you declare as an improvement for the rental side? What portion of your insurance have you charged off every year as expense for your rental? How much of your outside paint job?

I'll bet it was 50 percent, and if so, the IRS would say you long ago established only half of the building as your own residence.

Tax is due, by the way, on part of your profit, not on part of the selling price.

TAX BREAK ON COTTAGE

Dear Edith: My husband and I are going to sell a cottage we rent out this year and get the $125,000 tax break. Then we are getting a divorce and for my settlement he is signing the house we live in over to me. In a year or two later, can I get the $125,000 tax break also, selling the house as it would be in my name only then?—Mrs. C.D.

You'll still have that one-time $125,000 exclusion to use in the future, because you won't be able to apply it to the sale of the rental cottage. It is intended for one's primary residence only.

MARRYING BEFORE BIRTHDAY

Dear Edith: I will be 55 September 8. What I'd like to know, if I remarried before then, could I still sell my home and get the tax break? This man I know is 59 and he's already sold his house and used the tax break. I know that I would have to wait until I'm 55, right?—Ms. F.W.

Right. You must be 55 at the time of the sale, and you must not, on that day, be married to anyone who has ever used that exclusion (of up to $125,000 profit on the sale of a long-time principal residence).

Don't have the closing (settlement, transfer of title) before your 55th birthday, and don't marry before the closing date.

SELLING TWO RESIDENCES

Dear Edith: I bought a home up North in 1952. This is still our main residence. I bought a townhouse down South in 1968 for a winter residence for health reasons. Can I take the $125,000 tax exclusion on both homes if I sell them and buy something else?—Mr. H.P.

No.

The $125,000 exclusion is available only for profit on the sale of your one main home, known to the IRS as your principal residence, where you spend most of your time.

INTEREST AND THAT $125,000

Dear Edith: We recently sold our house at age 60. We will be paid $125,000 over a period of seven years, but $22,000 of that is interest on the loan we took back. Is the full $125,000 exempt from federal income tax?—Mrs. S.F.

Your profit on the sale of the house qualifies for the $125,000 exemption. Further interest the money earns will be subject to income tax. This is true whether the interest is earned through a mortgage loan, or on a CD at a bank.

MIXED UP ON TAX BREAKS

Dear Edith: I am still puzzled over this "over 55" tax break when selling one's principal residence, up to $125,000 tax-free profit. You keep saying (and I keep reading) "if you buy a more expensive residence within two years." What if we don't even buy another home when we sell our home of 27 years, but move to an apartment? Will you please straighten this out once and for all?—Mr. R.A.

You are confusing two different tax treatments for those who sell their own homes. The first allows sellers of any age to postpone tax on their profit if a more expensive replacement residence is bought within two years.

That's a postponement, not the tax exclusion you're asking about.

The other, different tax break is the chance for up to $125,000 profit free of any federal income tax ever. You use this only once, and you choose when you want to do it, any time after you're 55. You can use it whether you're buying another home or moving to an apartment. It has nothing to do with the other "replacement residence" regulation, except that it can stretch to include that postponed-tax profit on earlier residences.

PLOT OF LAND SALE

Dear Edith: I will be 75 years old in September. Does the over-55 tax break cover a plot of land sale (in the hopes that I can keep my own home of 46 years?) Thank you for an answer to this question. Sincerely—Mrs. S.G.

You will owe income tax on your profit from the sale of the land, whether or not you sell your home. The special tax breaks would apply only to your home itself on a normal house lot, not to surrounding acreage, and certainly not to land located elsewhere.

INTEREST IS TAXABLE

Dear Edith: An individual over 55 years of age sells his home on a 15-year land contract for deed arrangement. Is there any way that interest earned on this contract is eligible to be included in the $125,000 tax-free exclusion allowed for home sales? — Mr. A.Y.

No matter how you sell your home, interest earned by the proceeds is taxable as ordinary income. Principal received may sometimes qualify for one of the home-owners' tax breaks but interest it earns has no special tax status.

$38,000 ENTRY FEE

Dear Edith: I'm 67 and going to a retirement home in a few years. If I have to pay, say, $38,000 for entry fee before I sell my home, can I still take the special tax treatment when I sell my home? Even if I pay for the retirement apartment before I sold my home? — Mrs. B.I.

As you are over 55, if you've never used it before, you can claim that $125,000 profit exclusion from taxes when you sell your present home.

This has nothing to do with whether you have already bought into a retirement home or any other home. The exclusion will apply as long as the place you sold was your primary residence for at least three of the five years before you sold it.

FEDERAL OR STATE TAX?

Dear Edith: My sister is selling her home. She writes that her real estate broker says she will owe income tax on her profit, even though her husband is over 55. I told her about the one-time tax exemption you wrote about but her broker says it doesn't apply to residents of her state. Is this true? Please answer soon as I would like to show her your answer before settlement. — Mrs. D.P.

Your sister should seek tax information from an accountant or professional tax preparer, not from a real estate broker.

The chance to take up to $125,000 profit tax-free applies to federal income tax. Older residents of any state can take advantage of it when they sell a long-time home.

State income tax is something else. Some states follow the federal rules and allow the same exclusion. Other states do not.

If your brother-in-law is co-owner, if they've been living there at least three out of the past five years, and if neither of them ever took the exclusion before, it should be available for the federal income tax liability on their home.

MOTHER HASN'T PAID TAX

Dear Edith: In 1988 my mother sold her home. She is 92 years old and couldn't live alone any more. She did not pay any income tax for years, not having enough income. I know there is a one-time tax exclusion on selling your home but if you haven't paid income tax in years do you have to file for this exclusion?—B.D.

Your mother did have income in 1988 and should file a tax return. There may not be any tax after the exclusion is figured in, but the return is due.

Every real estate sale must be reported to the IRS by the person handling the closing, though that system isn't working perfectly yet. If your mother doesn't file a return, the IRS computer might go looking for it. Talk with a professional tax preparer. The procedure will be relatively simple.

NOT THERE THREE YEARS

Dear Edith: We have our house up for sale. I am 57 and I thought I could get the one-time tax break on capital gain. But now I have been told I have to be in the house for three years to get it. We have been here just two years.

Also my wife is under 55, so do I just claim one-half of the gain since it is joint?—K.T.

Only one of a couple need qualify to use that whole over-55 tax break, even if the house is jointly owned. But you don't qualify yet, because it must have been your primary residence for at least three of the five years before you sell.

Even if you can't use that one-time $125,000 exclusion, you will be eligible for the other home-seller's tax treatment, which allows you to roll over all or some of your profit and postpone tax if you buy a replacement primary residence within two years. Whether it covers your whole profit or only part of it depends on the relative sale prices of the two homes.

CANCELING THE EXCLUSION

Dear Edith: I am 67 years old. Last year I sold my home for $130,000, with a profit of $90,000. I took the one-time income tax exclusion. Then I bought a new home for $145,000. I am wondering if it would have been wiser to take the tax deferment instead since I'm not getting the benefit of the full $125,000 exclusion. I understand I can still amend my tax return. Your advice would be greatly appreciated.—Mrs. B.N.

Because the new home costs more than the last one sold for, you could indeed roll over your profit and postpone taxes. You have up to three years in which to amend your return and cancel your use of the one-time exclusion. You have nothing to lose.

DYING WITHOUT USING EXCLUSION

Dear Edith: I am 88 years old and eligible for the tax-free exclusion of $125,000 profit if I sell my home. My daughter age 67 is my sole beneficiary but never lived in this house. If I die still owning the house, would she get my exclusion?—Mrs. H.D.O.

No, but she wouldn't need it.

When she inherits your house, she gets it with what is called a stepped-up basis, as if she had bought it at current value. If she sold soon after, she'd have little or no taxable profit.

SOLD AFTER THE DIVORCE

Dear Edith: I sold my house in July, nine months after my divorce. I was 54 and my husband was 61. Can I take advantage of the $125,000 exclusion?—Mrs. M.A.

No, not this time around. In order to use that one-time exclusion, either you or your co-owning spouse must be 55 on the date of sale. On the date of sale, you weren't 55 and you did not have a spouse, so that's that. Perhaps you'll use that one-time tax break some time in the future, on another house.

ONLY ONE IS 55

Dear Edith: My husband and I will both be eligible for the $125,000 tax exclusion June when I also become fifty-five. Unfortunately, we will be transferred before May, and renting the house is out of the question. We must sell it. Last year, we read a tax booklet that said both of us must be age 55 and must have lived in the house three of the five years before the sale.

Is there any other way to avoid long-term capital gain tax other than to buy a house of equal value?—Mrs. I.L.

Either the booklet was wrong or you read it wrong. Only one of married co-owners need reach the age of 55 by the time of sale, to qualify for the tax break.

LETTERS I DIDN'T PRINT

Dear Edith: Please send me a copy of your leaflet on that $125,000 tax break on longtime home. Also question please. Can a 73 year old person have no limit on her income? Thank you.

Sky's the limit as far as I'm concerned.

Dear Edith: My house was sold due to a divorce which was my wife's wanting one for reasons not worth talking about unless it can save me money. My question is . . .

INGENIOUS PROPOSAL

Dear Edith: About the $125,000 exclusion article, you wrote about Mrs. T.K.N. who is 66 and can't get the exclusion because her husband had used it before they were married. Could this couple get a cheapie divorce, she sell the house and get the deduction and then they get remarried?

I'm afraid the IRS takes a dim view of divorces that are motivated for income-tax avoidance.

ACCOUNTANT'S BAD ADVICE

Dear Edith: When we wanted to move to a new house, our accountant told us to rent our old house out and wait until we were 55, then we could sell it and take our profit tax-free. But that was in 1984. Well, now we are over 55 but we don't meet the requirements for a tax-free sale (occupied the house for at least three of the five years before the sale.)

We lived in that house for 28 years. Can we still get the once-in-a-lifetime exclusion? — Mrs. E.P.

My guess is that the IRS isn't likely to make an exception for you. You could ask a lawyer if the accountant has any responsibility for bad advice. Then, of course, you might need to prove that's what the accountant said.

SELLING TWO LOTS

Dear Edith: Ten years ago we purchased two lots side by side in Florida for $7,800. We sold them last week for $32,000 for both. The commission fee was 10 percent. What federal and state income tax forms will we need to fill out when we file our tax returns? What are we allowed to deduct from the selling price? How do we figure how much tax we owe on the profit? — Mr. and Mrs. S.P.

You report the sale as a capital gain, on schedule D of your income tax return. You deduct commission and legal costs of selling, and of course your original cost. The rest represents profit.

GOOD NEWS ON THAT TAX BREAK

Dear Edith: We are in our 70s. We will probably now buy a mobile home with lot costing as much or more than we will get for this home. Any complications? — Mr. G.Y.

The mobile home qualifies as a replacement residence with the IRS. If it had kitchen and bath facilities, even a houseboat could qualify.

SELLING TWO HOUSES

Dear Edith: My husband and I would like to retire in a few years. We own the house we live in and another we moved from which is now rented. We would like to take the $125,000 one-time exclusion on each house when we sell them. I own them both. What if I transferred one to him, then he could sell one and I could sell the other?

Also, would there be taxes to be paid if I did transfer it to him? — H.B.

Property can be transferred between spouses with no federal tax consequences at all.

Doing so won't help, though. That "one-time" means just what it says. The tax break is for the sale of one's long-time principal residence, and you folks can have but one main home. (Even if you lived apart, it's still only one tax exclusion to a married couple.)

To accomplish what you want, you'd have to transfer the other house to your husband, have him move out and make the other house his main home for at least three years before he sold it, and get a divorce. Hardly seems worth it.

INDEX

A
Abstract, 98
Advertisements, understanding, 6
Age discrimination, 45, 103
Age, effect on mortgage qualification, 25, 29
Agent; *see also* Broker
    choosing, 3-4, 123
    compensation, 132
    gift to, 127-28
    license needed, 129, 131-32
    need for, 122
Appraisal, 70, 120
    FHA, 23
    vs. market analysis, 111
APR (annual percentage rate), 19, 53
Assessment, 117, 120
    vs. appraisal, 70
Attorney, 6, 7, 10, 91, 92, 97, 99, 130, 139, 145
    choosing, 104
    fees, 102
    in joint ownership, 15-16

B
Bankruptcy, effect on mortgage qualification, 27
Boundaries between properties, 97, 105
Broker; *see also* Agent
    avoiding a specific, 130
    buyer's, 3, 8
    choosing, 3
    commission, 163
    compensation of, 4, 7, 97, 110, 118, 122, 128-29, 130
    license needed, 129, 131-32
    need for, 109-10, 111
    responsibilities, 3, 7
Building inspection, 7
Buyer's broker, 3, 8
Buying "as-is," 7, 68-69

C
Child care, for real estate agents, 134-35
Children, discriminating against in renting, selling housing, 45
Closing costs, 4
    deductibility of, 60
Closing real estate sales 102-3
    walk-through at, 11
Commercially zoned property, selling, 116-17
Commission, 110-11, 118, 122, 126, 128-29, 130, 163
Condominium, regulations on length of rental, 46
Contract
    binding, 9-10
    release from, 10
    suggested provisions, 11
Creative financing, 6
Credit, 22
    counseling, 23, 26
    report, for tenants, 42-43

D
Deeds, 92, 93, 96, 97, 101
Defects, 7, 10-11

liability for, 66–70
Deposit, 9
Depreciation, 62
    effect on taxes, 33–35
Development, 9
Discrimination in renting, selling housing, 45, 103
Divorce, 100, 114, 147
    refinancing after, 145
    tax consequences, 160, 173
Down payment, 4, 6
    buying without, 19–20
    size of, 20

E

Engineering report, 7
Engineer's inspection, 121
Equity, borrowing against, 60–62
    in Texas, 62
Escrow, 56
Estate, sale of property by, 37
Estate taxes; *see* Taxes
Eviction, 47

F

Federal Housing Administration; *see* FHA
FHA; *see also* Mortgage, FHA
    function in mortgages, 22–23
    inspection, 68, 117
    mortgage insurance refund, 81–89, 144
    mortgage insurance refund, tracing, 86–88
Fixture, defined, 70
Florida, condominium regulations in, 46
Foreclosure,
    avoiding, 92, 95, 98
    effect on credit, 98
"For Sale" sign, 118
Fraud, 8, 21, 103

G

Gift letter, 22
Giving property to child
    problems, 78–79
    tax consequences, 148, 149
Government foreclosure sales, 38

H

Homebuying,
    new home vs. existing, 5
    out of local area, 4
    second thoughts after offer, 9
    timing, 3, 4
Home improvement, determining limits, 76, 77
Housing, shared, 72

I

Improvements, for selling, 110
Income and expenses, joint owners sharing, 15–16
Income, fluctuating, effect on mortgage qualification, 21
Inspection,
    at closing, 68
    engineer's, 121
    FHA, 68, 117
Insurance; *see also* Mortgage insurance
    homeowner's, 4
    title, 102
Interest, APR (annual percentage rate), 5
Investment
    financing, 35
    how to learn about, 37, 39
    no money down, 38
Investment property, repairs vs. improvements, defined, 62

K–L

Key, landlord's right to use, 44, 45
Kickback, 21, 128
    from seller, 8
Land contract, 98–99
Lease
    preparing, 42
    violations, 44
Lease-option, 46
Life estate, 93, 99
Life tenancy, 105
Listing for sale, 112, 126–27, 130
    canceling, 97
    open, 126
    term of, 126
L-V-R (loan-to-value ratio), 21

M

Market analysis, 111, 118
Marketing a house, 110
Mortgage
    adjustable rate, 18
    adjustable rate, index for, 54
    age as a factor in securing, 19
    amortization, 53
    assumability, 6, 112
    assuming, 142–43
    assuming, problems for original owner, 141–44
    escrow, 56
    Farmers Home Administration, 23–24
    Farmers Home Administration, refinancing, 24
    FHA, 19
    FHA, insurance, 55, 81–89
    FHA, using in another country, 30
    interest, 52
    interest rates, comparing, 19
    interest, tax deductibility of, 60, 63
    insurance, 55–56, 81–89
    insurance refund, FHA, 81–89, 144
    life insurance, 55–56, 82
    payment, analyzing, 12
    payments, accelerating, 52, 54
    payments, avoiding late charges, 135
    payoff, documents and recording, 74, 75
    payoff, early, discount for, 72–73
    payoff, early, pros and cons, 72
    payoff, problems, 139
    payoff, recording, 93–94
    points, 59–60, 116
    qualifying for, 19, 21, 22
    refinancing, 76
    refinancing, fees, 25–26
    sale of, 56–57
    second, 20
    "seller will hold," 6, 19
    shared-equity, 24–25
    types, 6, 17–18
    VA, 19
    VA, closing costs, 28–29
    VA, down payment, 28–29
    VA, foreclosure, 57
    VA, insurance, 55, 88–89
    VA, limits, 29–31
    VA, qualifying for, 28
    VA, refinancing, 76
    VA, refusal to accept, 30
    VA, using in another country, 30
    vs. cash, 17
Multi-family housing, as investment, 35–36
Multiple listing system, 126, 130

N–O

"No income verification" explained, 27
Offers, priority of, 7
Over-financing, problems, 36
Ownership
    establishing, 105
    joint, 15–16
    joint, ending, 16
    legal requirements, 92, 96, 99
    losing, 67–68

P

Partition, legal right of, 99
Physical condition, effect on mortgage qualification, 23
PITI (principal, interest, taxes, insurance), 20
PMI (private mortgage insurance), 18
    dropping, 54
Points, 4, 59–60, 116; *see also* Mortgage, points
Price, 5
    above asking, 8
    saving for full cash, 6
Pricing a house, 111–12, 113, 120, 121
Primary residence, defined, 168
Principals, defined, 6
Property taxes, deductibility of, 60
    liability for, 104
Purchase offer, VA rider, 29

R

Quit-claim deed, 101
Real estate career,
    age as a factor, 133
    part-time, 133
    training and education, 133
Rental, difficulties for absentee landlord, 35, 44, 77
Rental property, management, 48
Rent, requirement to pay far in advance, 47
Rents
    effect on income tax, 46
    setting, 44

Repairs vs. improvements, defined, 62
Retirement, selling in, 71, 72

S

Security deposit, getting back, 41
Seller financing, 135-39
    problems, 135-36, 140
Sellers, remaining in house after closing, 11
Selling
    commercially zoned property, 116-17
    for cash, 110
    getting advice from brokers, 119
    in retirement, 71, 72
    out-of-state, 112, 116, 118-19, 122
    timing, 115
    with furniture, 113
Selling and buying, order of, 114
Shared housing, 72
Small claims court, 67, 69
St. Joseph, 107-8
Subletting, damage during, 45-46
Survey, need for, 67
Survey stakes, moving, 100-101

T

Tax
    assessment, 117, 120
    return, reporting sales on, 155, 159, 172, 174
    sales, 36-37
Tax-deferred exchange, 154
Taxes
    deductibility of expenses on rental property, 60
    deductibility of interest, 147
    deductibility of mortgage interest, 60-61
    deductibility of points, 59-60, 63
    deferring by buying a new home, 157-61
    deferring by using former rental as a new home, 158
    deferring when moving out of country, 158
    effect of depreciation on, 33-34
    effect of rental income on, 34, 44
    estate, 77
    in negative amortization, 154
    one-time over-age-55 federal exclusion, 152, 154, 163-175
    one-time over-age-55 federal exclusion, after rental, 165
    one-time over-age-55 federal exclusion, canceling, 172
    on inherited property, 148-51, 152, 173
    on property received for services, 153
    on sale of second home, 148, 158
    property, 4, 60
    property, liability for, 104
    substantiating cost basis, 153
    timing sale in regard to, 153
    when depreciation has been taken on an office in the home, 161
    when new home costs less than old, 157
    when property is given to a child, 78-79
    when selling multi-family house owner lives in, 159, 170
Tenants
    credit report for, 42-43
    selecting, 42
Tenants' complaints, 48
Time-shares, 12, 13, 69
    reselling, 13
Title insurance, 102

V-W-Z

VA; *see also* Mortgage, VA
    eligibility, 28-30
    rider in purchase offer, 29
Value of property, 113, 114, 115, 120
Veterans Administration; *see* VA
Walk-through, at closing, 68
Will, effect of provisions on salability, 105
Zoning, changing, 95

KEEP YOUR COMPETITIVE EDGE WITH MORE BESTSELLERS FROM
REAL ESTATE EDUCATION COMPANY

	ORDER NUMBER	PRICE	QUANTITY	TOTAL AMOUNT
1. Classified Secrets: Writing Real Estate Ads That Work, 2nd Ed., by William H. Pivar and Bradley A. Pivar	1926-01	$ 29.95		
2. Close for Success: The Key to Real Estate Sales, by Jim Londay	1913-04	18.95		
3. Creative Real Estate Exchange: A Guide to Win-Win Strategies, by Milt Allen	1903-26	34.95		
4. Fast Start in New Home Sales, by Mark Seirsdale	1909-04	19.95		
5. Fast Start in Real Estate: A Survival Guide for New Agents, by Karl Breckenridge	1927-03	17.95		
6. How to Sell Apartment Buildings: The Big Money in Real Estate, by Gary Earle	4105-06	19.95		
7. Julie Garton-Good on Real Estate Finance—4 audio cassettes	1905-91	39.95		
8. The Landlord's Handbook: A Complete Guide to Managing Small Residential Properties, by Daniel Goodwin and Richard Rusdorf, CPM	4105-08	21.95		
9. List for Success, by Jim Londay	1913-01	18.95		
10. New Home Marketing, by Dave Stone	1909-03	34.95		
11. New Home Sales, by Dave Stone	1909-01	24.95		
12. Power Real Estate Letters: A Professional's Resource for Success, by William H. Pivar and Corinne E. Pivar	1926-03	29.95		
13. Power Real Estate Listing, 2nd Ed., by William H. Pivar	1907-01	17.95		
14. Power Real Estate Negotiation, by William H. Pivar and Richard W. Post	1907-04	19.95		
15. Power Real Estate Selling, 2nd Ed., by William H. Pivar	1907-02	17.95		
16. A Professional's Guide to Real Estate Finance: Techniques for the 90's, by Julie Garton-Good	1905-29	34.95		
17. Real Estate Prospecting: Strategies for Farming Your Markets, by Joyce L. Caughman	1913-07	24.95		
18. The Recruiting Revolution in Real Estate: Finding and Keeping Top-Quality Agents, by Carol Johnson	1978-02	34.95		
19. Staying on Top in Real Estate, by Karl Breckenridge	1927-04	18.95		
20. Successful Leasing & Selling of Office Property, 3rd Ed., by Real Estate Education Co. in conjunction with Grubb & Ellis Co.	1922-02	34.95		
21. Successful Leasing & Selling of Retail Property, 3rd Ed., by Real Estate Education Co. in conjunction with Grubb & Ellis Co.	1922-01	34.95		
22. Successful Real Estate Brokerage, 4th Ed., by Real Estate Education Co. in conjunction with Grubb & Ellis Co.	1922-03	34.95		
23. Winning in Commercial Real Estate Sales: An Action Plan for Success, by Thomas Arthur Smith	1922-05	24.95		

Shipping and Handling Charges:

Total Purchase:	Charge:
$ 0.00-24.99	$ 4.00
$ 25.00-49.99	$ 5.00
$ 50.00-99.99	$ 6.00
$100.00-249.99	$ 8.00

Orders shipped to the following states must include applicable sales tax: AZ, CA, CO, FL, IL, MI, MN, NY, PA, TX, VA, WI

Subtotal _____

Plus applicable sales tax _____
and shipping charges _____

Total _____

Order today! Call toll-free 1-800-621-9621 ext. 650. In Illinois call 1-800-654-8596 ext. 650 or use this order form and mail it to us.

Place your order today: Call toll-free 1-800-621-9621, ext. 650. In Illinois call 1-800-654-8596, ext. 650. Or fill out and mail this order form.

Real Estate Education Company • 520 N. Dearborn St. • Chicago, IL 60610-4975

Please send me the books indicated on the reverse side of this order form.

☐ Payment Enclosed

Charge to:

☐ Visa ☐ Mastercard ☐ Am. Ex.

Card No. _____

Exp. Date _____

Signature _____
(All charge orders must be signed.)

Name _____

Company _____

Street Address _____

City _____

State _____ ZIP _____

Business Phone (___) _____

830252

IMPORTANT - PLEASE FOLD OVER - PLEASE TAPE BEFORE MAILING

I understand that if I am not completely satisfied with my purchase, I may return it within 30 days for a full refund or credit.

IMPORTANT - PLEASE FOLD OVER - PLEASE TAPE BEFORE MAILING

Return address:
_____
_____
_____

Place Stamp Here

Real Estate Education Company
Order Department
520 North Dearborn Street
Chicago, IL 60610-4975